# MALIGN NEGLECT

## Misguided U.S. Foreign Policy in Latin America

The **Menges Hemispheric Security Project** of the **Center for Security Policy** Presents the Proceedings of:

The **Second Annual Capitol Hill National Security Briefing on Latin America,** Focused on Current Challenges to Democracy, Human Rights and Regional Stability in the Context of Threats to U.S. National Security

Thursday, April 22, 2010

Rayburn House Office Building

# MALIGN NEGLECT

## Misguided U.S. Foreign Policy in Latin America

Dr. Norman Bailey – Congressman Brian Bilbray – Gustavo Coronel – Douglas Farah

Dr. Luis Fleischman – Frank J. Gaffney, Jr. – Nancy Menges – Jon Perdue

Dr. Angel Rabasa – Ambassador Otto Reich – Congresswoman Ileana Ros-Lehtinen

Juan Carlos Urenda Diaz – Dr. Curtin Winsor, Jr.

**FRANK J. GAFFNEY, JR.**
*Publisher*

**ADAM SAVIT**
*Editor*

ISBN 978-0-9822947-8-9

PRINTED IN THE UNITED STATES OF AMERICA

1 2 3 4 5 6 7 8 9 10

FIRST EDITION

THE CENTER FOR SECURITY POLICY
1901 Pennsylvania Avenue, Suite 201
Washington, DC 20006
Phone: (202) 835-9077
Email: info@securefreedom.org

For more information, please see **securefreedom.org**

# Contents

# Introductory Remarks

**N**ANCY MENGES: Good morning. I would like to welcome all of you here to our second annual Congressional Conference on Latin America. We want to thank our congressional sponsors, Congressman Bilbray and Congressman Connie Mack for their support and their assistance. We also want to welcome members of the diplomatic corps representing countries from Panama, Spain, Nicaragua, El Salvador, and Venezuela.

The purpose of this briefing is to raise awareness of the dramatic changes that have taken place in Latin America over the course of the last ten years. Perhaps without our policymakers realizing it, the United States is slowly, but surely, being replaced by other countries such as China, Iran, and Russia as the dominant influence in the Western Hemisphere. Countries such as Brazil and Chile now have China as their major trading partner. Russia has sold billions of dollars of advanced weapons to Venezuela, and China recently made a commitment to loan twenty billion dollars to Venezuela to prop up its sagging economy and boost its oil production. Since coming to power eleven years ago, Venezuelan president, Hugo Chavez, has used his oil money to buy influence throughout Latin America and the Caribbean in a campaign to turn pro-American regimes against the United States.

We have learned from the laptop computer of Raúl Reyes, the slain leader of the FARC (Revolutionary Armed Forces of Colombia), that this narco-terrorist organization was actively operating inside Ecuador. Now firmly in the Chavista camp, President Correa of Ecuador refused to renew the lease on the American base at Manta last year. He, instead, has tried to negotiate a deal with a Chinese shipping company, Hutchison Whampoa, which has close ties to the People's Liberation Army. The Iranian government has been successful in establishing close relations with Venezuela, Bolivia, Ecuador, and Nicaragua and has found a warm welcome in Brazil. What this all means and how these various trends interconnect for regional stability and U.S. national security is the basis for our briefing today.

It is my pleasure to introduce our moderator, Frank Gaffney, the Founder and President of the Center for Security Policy, who has been a tireless leader, writer, and spokesman on behalf of the principles upon which this country was founded: freedom, democracy, and the rule of law. Frank Gaffney.

**FRANK GAFFNEY:** Thank you very much. I don't know whether she actually introduced herself. But that was Nancy Menges, who heads up the Menges Hemispheric Security Project at the Center for Security Policy. We are extraordinarily proud of this project, named for Nancy's late husband, Dr. Constantine Menges, a true guiding light for those of us in the field of national security in general and specifically with respect to hemispheric security which he knew a great deal about and was very passionate about. So it's a privilege to have Nancy working with us on this project and serving now as the driving force behind not just this event, but also a marvelous product called "The Americas Report," which is a go-to resource for what's happening in the hemisphere and documenting day-in and day-out some very significant trends that we will be discussing here today with an extraordinary group of experts in various fields, at the macro level, regional level, and hemispheric level and with respect to some of the key nations in the hemisphere.

This is the second annual hemispheric briefing by the Menges Project at the Center for Security Policy, and I'm sorry to say that the report this year is going to be worse than it was last year in a number of respects. We will be getting into that in detail in two very distinguished panels. But, before we do, we are very privileged to have with us, for at least a few minutes, leading members of the United States House of Representatives who have made this event possible through their sponsorship and who, through their leadership on these issues, offer us hope that the benign, or perhaps malign, neglect that has been applied to too much of the hemisphere for too long will yield to a much more thoughtful, much more engaged, and certainly much more responsible policy on the part of the United States.

# Congressional Remarks

**R**EP. ILEANA ROS-LEHTINEN: We have a motion to go into conference on our bipartisan Iran sanctions bill. The clock keeps ticking, Iran keeps spinning their centrifuges, and the U.S. is still trying to work out a deal with Russia and China; shame on us. But we finally have this motion on the floor today, so you'll excuse me in just a few minutes.

This Center does such incredible work, and one of the things that I always come away with when I look at what's going on in foreign policy is that, with this administration, it is better to be a belligerent enemy of the United States than a cooperative, close ally.

When you look at Syria, a country that sponsors extremist groups like Hezbollah and Hamas, what is our response to Syria? We sent them an ambassador, a U.S. ambassador, for the first time in five years.

And Israel, a close true ally, democratic ally of the Middle East, ally of our interests and our concerns, what do we do with Israel? We tell them to not build a condominium in Jerusalem, as if that is the single block that is stopping the Middle East peace process.

And we've seen what happens with the free trade agreements with Colombia and Panama. Can we get better allies than those two countries? Having been to Panama just recently, I can tell you that we've got not only two wonderful presidents in those countries, but also a wonderful community of people who love the United States in spite of the shabby treatment that we give them.

And look at what happened in Honduras. The U.S. called it a coup, even though the Honduran people went by their constitution. They went by their Supreme Court's decision. They abided by their rules, their laws, and the Micheletti government and the people of Honduras stood with us, in spite of the fact that we yanked their aid, including anti-narcotics aid, which is really the wrong type of aid to yank from a poor country like Honduras. And we took away their visas. And still, to this day, many individuals who were helpful in bringing democracy back to Honduras still have their visas revoked.

So that's how we treat Colombia, Panama and Honduras. And then you look at what's happening now, just today, these past few days, in Nicaragua. Just like Zelaya got away with what he was trying to do, Daniel Ortega is once again shining up his Sandinista medals and beating up the people who are crying out for true democracy and freedom in the country of Nicaragua.

So I thank this wonderful center because you always bring truth to what is going on in Latin America. The growing Iranian influence throughout the hemisphere, the flights that take place all the time between Tehran and Caracas should be a worry to anyone who cares deeply about our national security. Again, I thank the Center for what you're doing, and thank you so much, Frank and Nancy and Brian, for this opportunity.

**FRANK GAFFNEY:** Thank you, congresswoman. Good luck and Godspeed on your resolution. We appreciate you very much taking a few minutes to join us and for those words. Congressman Bilbray–Congresswoman Ros-Lehtinen has mentioned–is also a man deeply committed to our understanding of and addressing of problems south of our border, not least because of his very close scrutiny of what's happening on the border insofar as he represents the 50th district of California and has a personal history of living in immediate proximity to the border. This is a question not only of immigration and the implications of the dynamics of the turmoil in Latin America, but how these factors influence the flow of illegal aliens across our southern border.

Congressman Bilbray is the Chairman of the Immigration Reform Caucus in the House as well as a member of the Committee on Oversight in Government Reform. He is deeply involved in the debates that hopefully we will be contributing to in the course of the program today. Congressman Bilbray, again, thank you for your sponsorship of this event and for joining us. It was great to have you on Secure Freedom Radio yesterday to get a sense of the passion that you bring to this, and it's an appropriate scene-setter for what you'll be doing this morning. Again, thank you for joining us.

**REP. BRIAN BILBRAY:** Thank you. Ileana, thank you very much for your leadership on the committee. I know you have to move on that agenda, so please leave at your leisure. Let me just say, as somebody who literally grew up about two miles from *Avenida Revolución*, in my high school, you didn't worry about the drinking age in the United States, you just had to figure out how to catch a ride over to San Ysidro. But growing up with one foot on either side of the border–not just because the surf was better in Baja, but because our friends, the people I went to school with, were on both sides–the lack of perception or awareness the American people have of anything south of the border really frustrates me. The blind spot we have when it comes to Latin America is just so frustrating. I mean, people can tell you the history of the demise of the Austro-Hungarian Empire. They can talk to you about how Bismarck did this or that. But if you ask them, "When did Bolivar make his move? Where was he? What was going on?" You know, I always have to chuckle when I hear somebody talking about *Cinco de Mayo* as being "the independence day of Mexico," and it just boggles my mind that that type of ignorance has actually perpetuated in our culture. Not that it doesn't sell Corona beers, but anybody that's ever drank real Mexican beer knows how bad that stuff is.

My frustration is that this is not just an annoyance, this ignorance of the background of Latin America; it is a major threat to our community. And I see it as the greatest challenge that we have if we really want to talk about our grandchildren. What happens in Asia, what happens in Europe, and what happens in Africa gets a hundred times more attention than what happens in our own backyard. And it is almost like the old saying that if you want to hide something from someone, set it right in front of them because they'll look right over it. It frustrates me to see the kind of situations that go on with a total lack of awareness. If you ask the average American, "Why isn't the Shining Path included in the terrorist groups?" Well, nobody wants to bother about it. And also when you ask, "Why in the world would the United States stiff-arm one of its closest allies anywhere around the world?" We may not have been the parent of the country of Panama, but we were darn well the midwife. And for us to stiff-arm a nation that is that bonded to the American people, in history, in culture, and in economic balance just blows my mind. And it's so frustrating down the line. And when we see this kind of ignoring of the issues. A classic example: how many Americans know that there was talk of the whole issue of moving tanks to the border between Colombia and Venezuela? The aggressive actions taken by one country against another country in our own hemisphere, and most Americans don't even know about it or even care about it.

And then the issue in Honduras: there was a classic example where we preach and preach and preach that the politics of personality must be replaced with the politics of constitutional law. And you finally get a community, a nation that stands up for constitutional law. And we literally backhand them for doing it. We insult them. We attack them. To this day, we're still going at that, and I was just embarrassed as an American. I hate to say that. I don't say that very often. I'm a son of an immigrant. But I was embarrassed as an American to see how we treated Honduras during this issue. They stood up for constitutional law. They stood up to make this clear. It was a young congressman from Illinois that really has made a very interesting point about this. The administration said it wasn't going to recognize the election unless the previous executive was put back into office during that election, and the congressman from Illinois said, "Well, does that mean that in Illinois the federal government's not going to recognize our elections unless the governor gets reinstated into the position of executive branch?" And it really just showed the hypocrisy of the administration on this issue. And it's not just this administration. It's a real blind spot if not blatant ignorance of Latin America that frustrates me.

So those of us that think we're so sophisticated; I understand that there are a whole lot of things I don't know. But I think there are too many people in positions of power and influence, across the board, that are not smart enough to know what they don't know. They don't even perceive their ignorance. You can talk about the media that was hand-fed propaganda from down south. You can talk about the political process that followed that misinformation. And then you can talk about all these other issues where common sense will say, "These are the people we should be embracing. These are our hemispheric family members." And we should address that, because the threat coming out of our southern region is many times more of a threat than what we see from the Far East, Africa, or from Europe. And I think that it's time we start talking about that. I think the fact is that a lot of the problems that have originated in Latin America are now in our neighborhoods. Across the board. And it's not just one; it's multiple ones. The American community is becoming more aware of those and becoming more sensitive to the fact that they can see now in their neighborhoods the problems that have not been addressed on our southern frontiers or with our southern friends. That now is helping to bring the issue along from the American people's point of view. The trouble is the powers that be. Politics, media, economy–they tend to be way behind the American people on this issue, and I think you're going to see more and more American people saying, "Why aren't we taking care of a lot of these issues?"

Let me just say one thing, though; there are great heroes out there. I think that when we take a look at what happened in Honduras, you had not only people that were willing to stand up, but also people that were literally saying, "Do we need to stockpile eight months or ten months or a year of food?" We're talking about a nation that was looking to be starved out by the international community, including the United States. That is a sad thing that they're at that point because they stood up for the constitutional concept that their supreme court had impeached their president. And you can imagine if the world community was talking about doing that to us because we started the process against Richard Nixon. At the same time, though, there were heroes there and I want to give a plug for them. When the election came through in Honduras, the real hero was not the president who got elected, but the guy who lost. And I think we all ought to recognize that Mr. Santos stood up and he did more than almost anyone else in being able to make it clear to the world what the real issue was when he accepted the results of a free and open election. And I think that he's going to go down in history in Honduras as being the man who was in the right place at the right time with the right attitude.

Now we go over to the other challenges that we have, and we can talk about another hero. And he is the flipside of Zelaya and was a gentleman who was more popular than anybody else, who's done more for his country than we've seen in decades, if not centuries, standing up and taking on the drug cartels and the terrorists in Colombia. Everybody wants him to stay. Everybody is begging him to stay. President Alvaro Uribe was willing to stay, but the Supreme Court interpreted the constitution, and, as the great patriot he is, he accepted the constitutional limitations, and, no matter how much the public or he wanted him to continue, the constitution rules. And in Colombia, they have shown exactly how it's to be done. And I think that these two countries have shown other countries that are in crisis just exactly how to get the job done. And this may seem abstract when we talk about the realm of security, but this is the foundation of security, of constitutional legal process. Of governing from the book, not from the barrel of a gun.

And that is a real optimistic thing that I think we ought to recognize while we confront the challenges of trained terrorists being imported into South America. That people are literally modifying tanks in our own hemisphere so that they may be more available for invasion of a fellow country. These are challenges that we've got to look at; people looking at ways to be able to supersede the constitution and extend their authority, if not through electoral process, then through civil intimidation. All of these are realities that we have down there. But I just want to thank you very much for being able to get together this morning and talk about this, because I think that all around America we need to talk more about these issues; that there are spheres of influence that we need to address. And I for one have to say that Africa is not our backyard. Europe should be taking a lead there. We should be supporting them, but we should not be the lead agency there. That's not our backyard. Asia is very important, but it's not our backyard. We should not be the lead agency there. We should be supporting.

But our own hemisphere, this is where we should take the lead. We should be putting the emphasis here, and this is where other power bases should support us, in this hemisphere. And we should be working one on one with our neighbors to the south, making sure that this hemisphere has the ability to have that dialogue. And rather than it being a backwater–from the aspect of political, social and news media attention–it should be the front page of every politician's speech and the front page in every newscast. And sadly that's not true right now, and, until we do that, the threats that exist in our own hemisphere are not going to be addressed in an appropriate manner. But this is a step and I want to thank you very much for allowing us to participate.

# Panel One

## INTERNAL SECURITY, ASYMMETRIC WARFARE, CHAVEZ'S HOUSE OF CARDS AND IRANIAN PENETRATION

**FRANK GAFFNEY:** We're going to turn now to an extraordinary panel to talk about what I think of as "macro issues" in the hemisphere. It's a time of considerable ferment, considerable dynamism, and considerable areas that are manifestly of concern to those who love freedom. The congressman has pointed to several very hopeful developments, specifically the triumph of freedom in Honduras against long odds and the respect for the constitution in Colombia. And it will be with those hopeful signs very much in mind that we will turn to some of the signs that are not quite so hopeful.

*Moderated by* **Frank J. Gaffney, Jr.:** President and Founder, the Center for Security Policy. *This discussion included:* **Dr. Luis Fleischman:** Senior Academic Advisor, the Menges Hemispheric Security Project; **Jon Perdue:** Director of Latin American Programs, the Fund for American Studies; **Gustavo Coronel:** former Venezuelan congressman; **Dr. Norman Bailey:** President of the Institute for Global Economic Growth.

We're going to be hearing from four experts in this first panel, both with respect to their topics and more generally with respect to the hemisphere. I'll introduce each of them in turn, and then we'll go through the list and I'll recognize them to take up the cudgel. I'm going to ask each of them to respect the ten minute rule here in the Congress, and thereby we'll hopefully have some time for questions from you all.

Our first speaker will be **Dr. Luis Fleischman**. We are very proud that he is a Senior Academic Advisor to the Center for Security Policy's Menges Hemispheric Security Project. He is also an adjunct professor at the Wilkes Honors College at Florida Atlantic University. Luis will be speaking about the very important relationship between the sorts of internal developments that we'll be talking about this morning, throughout the region and the security of the region more generally. He'll be followed by **Jon Perdue**, the Director of the Latin America Programs at the Fund for American Studies. Jon is an expert on many issues in this region, but he will be speaking to us today about asymmetric warfare. It's growing use, both in Central and South America, and its implications for all of us. Jon will be followed by **Gustavo Coronel**, one of the folks who has fled Hugo Chavez's Venezuela. He is a geologist, political scientist, was formerly on the board of PDVSA, and also served as a Venezuelan congressman. So welcome to our Congress, congressman. You will be speaking about the rise and fall of the Bolivarian Revolution. That actually sounds rather hopeful, so we'll look forward to that. And then the cleanup batter for this first panel will be **Dr. Norman Bailey**, a friend and colleague of mine for many years. He served with great distinction on President Reagan's National Security Council and was instrumental to many of the very important things that were accomplished during that presidency. It is great to have you with us. He is now a consulting economist, the President of the Institute for Global Economic Growth, and also a member of the faculty at the Institute of World Politics. And Norman will be speaking about an issue that was touched on by Congresswoman Ros-Lehtinen; the growing Iranian presence in Central and South America and what it means for the region and for us. So with that, Luis, welcome and ten minutes.

**DR. LUIS FLEISCHMAN:** Thank you, Congressman Brian Bilbray and Congressman Connie Mack, for co-sponsoring this event, and also to Frank and Nancy and the Center for Security Policy for putting this wonderful event together. Many thanks to Congressmen Bilbray and Ileana Ros-Lehtinen for their excellent presentations.

A large part of the Latin American continent today is in danger of falling into a situation that fluctuates between totalitarianism and anarchy and between authoritarianism and chaos. The region is also in danger of falling under the influence of insurgent and terrorist groups, drug cartels, and distant countries that historically have been poles apart from the region's culture and civilization, like Iran, China, and Russia.

These events cannot be understood without understanding the presence and expansion of the Bolivarian Revolution. In this presentation, I will try to bring some insight into the implications of such a combination of factors for the region and try to anticipate some future scenarios in terms of national and regional security.

Venezuela, under Hugo Chavez, established a model of government and ideology that has implications on domestic as well as on foreign policy. Both domestic and foreign policy are related. Domestically, there is an attempt to impose the Bolivarian Revolution, which is a sort of absolute socialism. Bolivarianism attacks private property, and the market. Likewise, it suppresses the civil and political opposition and the freedom of expression. It has also subjugated the judiciary to presidential prerogatives. In terms of foreign policy, Hugo Chavez is trying to expand his revolution throughout the continent in order to impose his own hegemony as opposed to that of the United States. So domestically the model of Hugo Chavez, of suppression of civil society and political society, is being introduced in the countries that follow the Chavista model. These are mainly Ecuador, Bolivia, and Nicaragua. My guess is that other countries may follow. So under the veil of pursuing social justice, Chavez and his allies have sought to strengthen and perpetrate executive power by using the momentary popularity of the president. Thus, they proceeded to carry out a constitutional reform to do so. Such a model of concentration of authority in the hands of the president and internal suppression also has implications for foreign policy. This is because the expansion of the Chavez revolution in the region can be done only by talking to a handful of regional leaders who are not accountable, neither to congress, nor to public opinion, nor to civil society in general. Hugo Chavez is also trying to reach out to grassroots and indigenous movements in order to incorporate them into his Bolivarian Revolution. However, Chavez will not wait for these movements to support him and give him legitimacy; he is a true revolutionary. The use of violence is crucial for every revolutionary movement.

Therefore, there is no better ally for Hugo Chavez than the Revolutionary Armed Forces of Colombia, also known as the FARC. The FARC is currently being defeated in Colombia. As the FARC is being defeated, it's moving to other countries. For instance, in Ecuador and Bolivia, there is already a strong presence of FARC militants. The FARC no longer, in my opinion, will be a pure movement trying to change the situation in Colombia. At this point, in my view, it has become part of the Bolivarian Revolution. To confirm this, there is a new group that FARC and Chavez created together called the Bolivarian Continental Coordinator, or CCB. The CCB met two months ago and the members of the Basque guerilla group, ETA, and others participated. It is obvious to me that the aim of the CCB is to spread and promote insurgency across Latin America on behalf of the Bolivarian Revolution. Of course there is the possibility that Middle Eastern groups could join that particular activity of promoting insurgency.

Another point I want to stress here is the nature of the relationship between the Bolivarian Revolution and the drug cartels. The drug business has always existed, but, according to a report published last year by the Government Accountability Office, Venezuela has helped extend the lifeline to drug cartels. At this point, the flow of cocaine transiting from Venezuela to the United States, Europe, and West Africa increased more than four times between 2004 and 2007, and it continues to sharply increase. At this point, drug trafficking continues to expand all across Latin America; including Central America, Ecuador, Bolivia, and Peru. The importance of the drug business is not simply that it is a criminal activity that affects our citizens; it corrupts the institutions of the state and undermines the authority of the state. Drug money can buy lawyers, judges, policemen, politicians, everything. This is further aggravated by the fact that Bolivia, Ecuador, and Venezuela expelled the Drug Enforcement Administration from their countries. There is no better example to show what the drug business can do than by looking at Mexico and Guatemala. In the Mexican states that border with the U.S., there is no real distinction between police members and members of the drug cartels. In other words, the police have been largely taken over by drug cartels. In Guatemala, people hire private security companies because the regular authorities cannot exercise control over what is called "the monopoly of the means of violence."

So what is being created on the continent and stimulated by Chavez is a situation of anarchy; a situation similar to the one that is being experienced by Afghanistan today. In Afghanistan, like in parts of Latin America, the authority of the state is weak and the power is in the hands of non-state groups or warlords. This situation can perpetuate itself even if Chavez were to disappear. In other words, even if Chavez is gone tomorrow, this situation of "Afghanization" is already a situation that should be of deep concern for the United States. This is particularly important given what is happening in our own backyard. Chavez is likely to promote this kind of situation and take advantage of this state of anarchy and instability in order to push those countries toward the Bolivarian Revolution.

Obviously this situation makes it easy for groups such as the pro-Iranian Hezbollah and others to penetrate the region. There is already cooperation between Hezbollah and Mexican drug cartels. Mexican drug cartels have access to the southern border of the United States, so this cooperation represents a real danger to American security. Hezbollah can take advantage of this to harm the United States. In addition, young Venezuelans are being trained in Hezbollah camps in southern Lebanon. That was reported about a year ago. This is extremely important because members of Hezbollah, Hezbollah-trained Venezuelans, or even Iranian revolutionary guards–whose presence was recently reported by the Pentagon–could play a role in preserving the totalitarian nature of Chavez and his allies' regimes. Remember, there is a new law today in Venezuela that establishes a militia–a militia above the army. This militia, according to the law, may include Venezuelan-born or foreign-born people. Now, if that is the case, it should not be ruled out that the militia could be composed of members of the FARC, Middle Eastern groups, and other dangerous groups.

In regard to Iran, there is the issue of Iran's advancement towards acquiring nuclear weapons. Venezuela and Iran are close allies, and Venezuela has become one of Iran's staunchest supporters. Chavez has facilitated its banking system to Iran and reportedly has also produced uranium for Iran. So what is Chavez going to ask from Iran in return? I think what we should not rule out is the possibility that once Iran becomes nuclear–and that's a possibility–Venezuela will become nuclear. This development could be very worrisome, particularly when Venezuela is arming itself and promoting antagonism with Colombia. At this point, the Venezuelan army is no match for Colombia. Therefore, in this context, it makes sense for Chavez to pursue nuclear weapons.

I have two more points, but I think I'm going to defer them to the question and answer period. I'd be happy if you could ask me later. Thank you so much.

**FRANK GAFFNEY:** We will try to insure that there is time to ask what it is he didn't get to say. But thank you very much for what you did say, Luis. Jon Perdue on the growing asymmetric warfare in Central and South America. Welcome.

**JON PERDUE:** Thanks, Frank. For those of you that saw the Bill Gertz piece yesterday in the *Washington Times* about Iran expanding the number of Quds Force in Venezuela, it presents a really good lead-in into what I want to talk about this morning, asymmetric warfare, or what the estimable Max Manwaring calls "Fourth Generation Warfare." And this morning, in the *Washington Times*, there was also a new article about the fact that, after a year and a half of the hopeful new diplomacy of constructive engagement, Hezbollah now has SCUD missiles. The Obama administration had been working for a full year and a half to convince Syria–by force of personality, I would assume–to not give SCUD missiles to Hezbollah. So I fear that that might be a leading indicator of what may come to be the result of this type of foreign policy. It's like the theory of third marriages: the triumph of hope over experience. Or is it second marriages? Maybe so.

Ever since the Iran/Iraq war, Iran has focused not on building up their conventional forces, but on (1) building up the navy so they can cause havoc within the Persian Gulf region, and on (2) expanding their proxy forces, which is mainly the Quds Force, the IRGC, Hezbollah, and Hamas. And what this allows them to do is affect other nations, affect their enemies in the region, and affect their allies in Latin America, for instance, who are also their allies against the United States, in ways that allow them to maintain plausible deniability. In the Bill Gertz piece yesterday, there were declassified documents that talked about the expansion of the Quds Force in Venezuela. And, although I hate to read rather than to speak extemporaneously on this, I think to get the detail of some of these documents I'm going to have to.

Let me say, above all else, the tactics of asymmetric warfare that they are using are designed to propagate the survival of the regime. And that goes for Iran, of course, as well as Chavez and Daniel Ortega, for instance, which we will get a really good glimpse of in the upcoming Nicaraguan elections, as well as Ecuador and Bolivia and hopefully not too many others in the near future.

The method of utilizing proxies and gaining perimeter footholds has been the *modus operandi* of Iran and its arms-length war with Israel. Since Ahmadinejad was elected in 2005, he has consolidated power in Iran by utilizing the Basij militia to suppress opposition while embedding the Revolutionary Guard with more positions within the government and its bureaucracies. Since the end of the Iran/Iraq war, Iran decided not to develop a conventional force structure.

Similarly, after narrowly surviving a coup in 2002, Hugo Chavez first purged his military of any soldiers that appeared supportive of the coup and soon after began to indoctrinate his military in asymmetric warfare. At the first military forum on asymmetric war in 2004, Chavez instructed his soldiers to change their tactical thinking from a conventional style to a "people's war," which glorified the tactics used by revolutionary Islamists.

Chavez then had a special edition of *Peripheral Warfare and Revolutionary Islam* printed in Spanish and distributed to the Venezuelan army to replace the U.S. Army Training Manual. This new training manual idolizes Islamic terrorism, calling it the ultimate and preferred method of asymmetric warfare because it involves fighters willing to sacrifice their lives to kill the enemy. The manual also contains instructions for making and deploying a dirty bomb. I brought copies with me–at least I printed as many copies this morning as my printer would put out before it surrendered–but I underlined in the copy of the manual where it shows how to make a dirty bomb and I want to–well, I'll cover that in a minute at the end of the presentation.

This peripheral warfare strategy was road-tested in Iran in its 2006 proxy war with Israel, when two of its surrogate forces, Hezbollah and

Hamas, utilized special missile crews to bomb Israeli citizens as well as to cause distraction when it fired upon Israeli border patrols to start the Israel/ Hezbollah War. Even prior to the U.S. decision to remove Saddam Hussein in 2003, Iran was perfecting the use of peripheral warfare by supplying and training Shi'ite groups in Iraq.

Iran also used this strategy against Egypt when it built up a presence just south of its border with Sudan in order to support terrorist operations against Hosni Mubarak's government. And it also helps subversive groups in Yemen that could threaten Saudi Arabia's oil structure.

In April of 2009, Egypt arrested members of a Hezbollah cell consisting of Egyptians, Lebanese, and Palestinians that were smuggling arms to Hamas. A week later, Egypt arrested four agents from the Iranian Revolutionary Guard Corps that had been sent to Egypt to set up an intelligence network.

Egypt, a longtime foe of Iran, had to contend with its own potential insurgency via the Muslim Brotherhood, which also has close ties to Hamas. The major difference between Iran's use of peripheral warfare in the Middle East and Venezuela's is that the latter can much more easily find allies in the region willing to overtly offer support, whereas Iran must maintain some semblance of plausible deniability in its subversive activities.

The correspondingly lesser scrutiny and import given to Latin America allows Chavez to openly tout his Bolivarian Revolution throughout the region. Aside from the use of ALBA (Bolivarian Alliance for the Americas) houses, peripheral warfare conducted by Hugo Chavez has included setting up the Venezuelan Information Office here in Washington and hiring PR firms to improve his image in the U.S. One of the propaganda coups has been the notorious campaign with Joseph Kennedy, and some of you have probably seen these commercials about supplying cheap heating oil to down-and-out New Englanders who enjoy a standard of living only dreamed about by poor Venezuelans who suffer constant electricity and food shortages on top of the newly-devalued currency.

The exclusivity of Chavez's access to oil has allowed him to subvert corrupt politicians in the region as well as to offer a sanctions-busting 20,000 barrel-a-week deal to Iran. But it's this benign neglect policy of the United States toward Venezuela that may also end up being the very thing that entices Chavez to overstep.

My favorite quote of Hugo Chavez is, "I will put my enemy to sleep so that one day he will wake up dead." These subtle subversion measures are designed to gain a military or propaganda advantage without provoking a response from a superior enemy. What we are really talking about is what is our "threshold of concern?" That's a phrase that's often used by diplomatic experts–what is the United States' "threshold of concern" or how much can be gotten away with before we react? What we are really talking about as a "threshold of concern" is what line must be crossed before we're no longer able to choose to respond as an act of prevention, but we instead are forced to respond as an act of retaliation.

One of the things that Doug Farah talked about at this event last year was the "pipeline" that runs from, let's say, Tierra del Fuego all the way to the Rio Grande or the Gulf of Mexico. But you could put any inert object, let's say, in the tri-border area of Paraguay, Brazil, and Argentina–or a person, let's say, a live or inert object–and it will get to its destination basically with the reliability of FedEx or UPS here in the United States. And as Luis mentioned, that when Iran goes nuclear, which looks more and more inevitable as we go along, it's a good possibility that Venezuela may as well.

And I think that as we get closer to having to act against a nuclearized Iran, one of the possibilities may not be an al-Qaeda type attack on the United States, but you could send, let's say, a Venezuelan, a Nicaraguan, and a Cuban to the tri-border area. Train them there and send them up the pipeline–one to Tijuana, one to Matamoros, and one to Fort Hancock, Texas. Get them across the border and set off a dirty bomb in the remote desert. No deaths. No casualties. But it's a signal, and it will let the United States know that if we attack Iran, or even if Israel attacks Iran, a dirty bomb will go off in the center of Los Angeles or New York.

In the interest of time, I'll stop on that optimistic note and elaborate in the question and answer session if necessary. Thank you.

**FRANK GAFFNEY:** Jon, thank you. The complexities and challenges of asymmetric warfare are clearly something we've got to be focused on. Gustavo Coronel, former member of congress in Venezuela, will tell us about the rise and–from your lips to God's ears–fall of the Bolivarian Revolution.

**GUSTAVO CORONEL:** Thank you. Good morning to everyone. As you know, Chavez came into power eleven years ago. And he came into power because he promised to eliminate corruption in Venezuela. Of course, corruption in Venezuela nowadays is the most intense we have ever had, so he failed in his main electoral promise. There are two problems with the name he gives his movement. He calls it the "Bolivarian Revolution." The first problem is that it is not Bolivarian, and the second is that it is not a revolution. A revolution, of course, is a radical change, hopefully, to improve things. But in his case, there has been a radical change to make the country worse than ever before.

Chavez has developed a political model, key strategies, and some main tactics. The political model is almost identical to the one Fidel Castro developed in the 1960's. It has to do with (1) authoritarian rule at home, (2) trying to become a hemispheric leader and, (3) the leader of a global anti-U.S. alliance. In turn, his strategies are based on three pillars: (1) oil money–he has had so far no less than nine hundred billion dollars of income in eleven years, (2) the support of the armed forces, which are co-opted and are being supplied with abundant privileges and money by Chavez, and (3) a real following among the poor. Many of the poor support Chavez because Chavez has expressed interest in the poor. But, of course, if you consider Venezuela as if it were a bus, what he has done is to put the poor into the bus, but at the expense of expelling the middle class from the bus. And that, of course, is no solution. You cannot include a sector of the population at the expense of excluding another sector of the population.

His main tactics have had to do with handouts at home and abroad. In fact, as the old Chinese proverb goes, his policy is one of giving fish but not one of teaching anyone how to fish. And, as you can imagine, when the fish runs out, people getting fish will be more dependent on the paternalistic government and more defenseless than ever before. He has given money abroad. About thirty-five to forty billion dollars has been given to his friends–ideological friends in Latin America. He has been working within OPEC to try to reduce oil production so that oil prices increase. He has been financing the extreme left in Latin America and in almost every country, including Peru, Argentina, and Chile. Five of his ambassadors have been expelled from these countries because of their open intervention in their internal affairs. He has been aligning himself with rogue states all over the world. His club now includes Iran, Syria, Libya, and Cuba–all the "good" guys. And finally, he has done quite a lot of recruiting in the U.S., especially in Hollywood, where he has become the favorite dictator.

Now, what are the results of these strategies and his tactics? Number one: he's still popular. He's currently at forty percent popularity. This is still very high, except that before, a few years back, he had seventy percent popularity. Two: he has gained influence in Latin America and the Caribbean by giving oil to the small countries which import oil. Three: he has converted Venezuela into the preferred ally–and I would say almost the only ally–of Iran. He has made inroads in the United States. You listen to Joseph Kennedy II and he's very enthusiastic about Chavez. Or you listen to certain sectors of the academic world in the U.S. and they are also very enthusiastic. Hollywood's Danny Glover received 18 million dollars to make a picture that he will never finish.

Chavez has also become very influential in the OAS. Not only because he has acted very shrewdly, but because Insulza has been a disaster as a secretary general. In OPEC, he has not made any inroads because Saudi Arabia is the leader. So he doesn't control how the production can increase or diminish. In the Latin American region, he has done quite a lot of work proselytizing in the small Caribbean countries through his PETROCARIBE initiative. That means oil in exchange for bananas and black beans and that sort of thing.

Now, what is the outlook? Eleven years later the revolution is stagnant. He can no longer win in his original conception of winning. Now he's surviving. He can no longer make Venezuela into another Cuba. He can no longer make the region into a socialist bloc. Oil money now is less abundant than before, and that means losing friends; friends are there as long as money is there. The currency has been devalued. There is a tremendous electricity crisis in Venezuela. There are food shortages. The crime rate is the highest in the hemisphere. We have sixty violent deaths per one hundred thousand inhabitants in Venezuela, even more than El Salvador and Mexico. So we are now witnessing what is an impending implosion of the so-called "revolution." High-level followers have been leaving him. The vice president left and he took his wife along because his wife was a minister. He has already lost several ministers and a key governor in the state of Lara to the opposition. In fact, he lost an entire political party. PPT, *Patria Para Todos*, is no longer a Chavez follower. They have abandoned him. And the whole regime seems to be crumbling down. The polls show that his popularity has been highly diminished. So my outlook, or my prediction if you wish, probably with a small component of wishful thinking, is that Chavez will not finish his term in 2012. He will be ousted before 2012. Thank you.

**FRANK GAFFNEY:** Thank you, Congressman. That is, as I said, I hope not so much wishful thinking but accurate forecasting. But we appreciate very much your background on how some of these trends are working within Venezuela. It certainly informs us on the rest of the region as well. We come now to Dr. Norman Bailey. We'll hear a bit more about that Iranian presence that Jon talked about and how its techniques of asymmetric warfare are playing a growing role in both Central and South America. Dr. Bailey.

**DR. NORMAN BAILEY:** Thank you very much, Frank and Nancy, and good morning to everyone. In February of last year, I traveled to New York to brief the staff of the district attorney of Manhattan and the New York Federal Reserve Bank on the Iranian situation in Latin America. Subsequently, District Attorney Morgenthau, as one of his last acts before retiring at the age of ninety at the end of last year, did an extraordinary thing. He came to Washington in September and warned the U.S. government, the public, and the media about Iranian penetration into the Western Hemisphere. He might just as well have thrown his talk into the Hudson River or the Potomac for all the good that it did in terms of anybody taking any action as a result. In any case, the presentation that I made at that time has gone through various versions since then, and the most recent version was published last month by the University of Miami's Center for Hemispheric Policy as part of their series on challenges to security in the Western Hemisphere Task Force of which I was a part. And it's entitled, "What Are the Persians Doing Over Here?"

Remarkably little attention has been paid to this, and yet I will make the case that Iranian involvement in the Western Hemisphere is a direct threat to the national security of the United States, whereas Chinese and Russian involvement, although contrary to the national interests of the United States, is not a direct threat to the national security of the United States. There has been some work done on it. One good report was done by Douglas Farah. And one of the best, as a matter of fact, was done by an Israeli analyst. Then there is Morgenthau's own talk, and most recently the Woodrow Wilson Center published a monograph on the subject.

I'm going to talk just very briefly about the involvement of Iran in the Western Hemisphere outside of Venezuela and then I'm going to devote most of my time to its involvement in and through Venezuela. Iran opened an embassy in Nicaragua, and it has a large staff made up of agents of the Iranian security and intelligence forces. Their area of operation is Central America and most notably Panama. Iran has done various deals with Ecuador–has "signed" various deals, I should say, rather than "done" various deals, because the Iranians are famous for signing things and promising things and then not doing them. But then they get the credit for them because when they sign them, you have publicity; newspaper, television, and so on. The fact that they never follow through does not get into the publicity machine. But the most interesting thing in Ecuador is that recently many of the financial activities of Iran, which are used to evade financial sanctions on the part of the U.S., the EU, and the UN, have moved from Venezuela, where they have been attacked–particularly by the United States Treasury Department, the only agency of the United States government that has been active in opposing Iranian penetration–and have moved to Ecuador. Various deals have been signed with Bolivia. Recently, uranium mining exploration deals were signed with Guyana in return for money. The Guyanese could do it only by violating a contract they had with a Canadian company to explore the same region. Then there is Argentinean involvement in the tri-border area where Hamas, Hezbollah, and Islamic Jihad have raised money primarily. And the most interesting thing outside of Venezuela, as far as I'm concerned, is the developing love affair between President Lula of Brazil and President Ahmadinejad of Iran. I think this is very significant. It's very interesting. President Lula, during his administration, has followed what I call the PRI pattern. That is conservative internally, radical externally, and then you keep the left happy because you're doing radical things externally, while, in fact, you're governing in a rather conservative fashion. And that is extremely unhelpful to the United States.

Venezuela. I've already mentioned about finance. The Iranians have set up various financial institutions in Venezuela, which are used for the purpose of evading financial sanctions, and these have been sanctioned by the Treasury Department.

Industrial–including nuclear–Venezuela has signed deals with Iran, as well as Russia, to develop nuclear power. As far as industrial installations are concerned, there is a map in the report which shows how widespread these installations are throughout Venezuela. There are tractor factories, cement factories, and all kinds of other factories that have been set up by the Iranians. The only problem is that the tractor factory doesn't make tractors and the cement factory doesn't make cement. The tractor factory makes weapons and the cement factory is used for the export of cocaine. A cement plant is the perfect warehouse for cocaine because the powder looks like cement, is packed in bags that say "cement," and is then exported as cement. And it is exported largely by a fleet of oceangoing tuna boats, which are a perfect way to transport cocaine because the tuna's on top, the cocaine is underneath, and the smell of the tuna masks the cocaine. And then it goes over to West Africa and is transshipped to Europe.

Transportation. There are weekly flights between Caracas and Tehran, stopping in Damascus. Half of these flights are Venezuelan airliners, and half are Iranian airliners. The only problem with these "commercial" flights is that you can't buy passage on them. If you go into the office in Caracas and say, "I want to go to Damascus," or "I want to go to Tehran," they say, "Wonderful, go someplace and make an arrangement." You say, "Well, wait a minute, don't you have a flight leaving on Wednesday?" They say, "Yes, but it's full." It's always full. It's permanently full. And since the Venezuelan government has expropriated all the ports and airports of the country, there is no way of penetrating the dense fog that covers their operations. And these flights. The people on these flights do not go through customs, they don't go through immigration, and they don't go through any bureaucratic procedures whatsoever. But the cargo area is always full. The Iranians and the Venezuelans have set up a joint shipping company. Then, when the United States sanctioned that, they simply changed the name and set up another shipping company and so forth. And the Turks intercepted a shipment that was marked "tractor parts," which turned out to be parts of weapons and materials to make explosives and other weapons.

Energy. The Iranians and the Venezuelans are great allies in OPEC and otherwise, and the Iranians have been given areas in Venezuela for exploration.

Drug trafficking I've already mentioned, and a lot of the drug trafficking is used to finance the activities of Hezbollah, Hamas, and FARC through their installations in Venezuela.

Proselytization among indigenous groups. The Wayuu tribe has become Shi'a Islam. That tribe is on the border between Venezuela and Colombia, which makes it very useful for various purposes. I've already mentioned support of Hezbollah and Hamas.

Now, why is Iran doing all of this since, in the entire five thousand year period of the Persian Empire, there has been absolutely no interest whatsoever on the part of Persia/ Iran in the Western Hemisphere until recently? I put it on the table that it is to make it possible for Iran to retaliate against the United States if it is attacked by the United States or by Israel.

Recommendations. One: put certain Venezuelan banks and some of their affiliates on the sanctions list. Two: declare Venezuela a state sponsor of terrorism so that certain actions can be taken, particularly boycotting Venezuelan oil exports to the United States. Simultaneously with this action it should be announced that an equivalent amount of crude oil will be released from the Strategic Petroleum Reserve (SPR) for the time necessary for the market to adjust to the measure. The oil in the SPR is in any case of superior quality. And, at this point, Venezuelan shipments to the United States are only about eight hundred and fifty thousand barrels a day. Three: patrol the mouth of the Orinoco River because that's where most of the drugs go out, and they go directly out into the Atlantic, not into the Caribbean. Four: monitor much more closely Iranian activities in all the areas outlined above as well as in other parts of the continent, particularly Panama.

And Mr. Chairman, I return back the remaining five seconds of my time.

**FRANK GAFFNEY:** The balance of your time. An exercise in discipline that is most appreciated. Thank you to all of the panelists for making their remarks within the allotted time, with the exception of Luis, who kindly yielded his back without having finished his remarks. Let me just, if I may, ask if there is something you wanted to say on Russia and China that we could just quickly introduce, and then we'll open it up to the rest of the audience.

**DR. LUIS FLEISCHMAN:** Thank you, Frank. I think, Norman, you said that China is not really a significant threat. I agree that it is not a direct threat, but it is an indirect threat. At this point, China is increasing investments in Latin America by four hundred percent, and that increase has been tremendous, particularly in the last two years, from 2007 to 2008. A Chinese company actually controls the Panama Canal. In addition, China is taking over what the U.S. left vacant in Manta after it was expelled by Ecuadorian President, Rafael Correa. So as China enjoys such economic and political leverage, this could help perpetuate Chavez and his allies. In addition, I want to remind the audience what scholar Larry Diamond has said. Diamond pointed out that democracy is in trouble today because China's economic growth and increasing influence in the world enables it to support and even bail out authoritarian regimes. China is not interested in democracy, and is less interested in being pressured to democratize. Therefore, China will tend to support these authoritarian regimes. The same thing could apply to Russia whose relations with Chavez and his allies are increasing too. If Russian President Dmitri Medvedev follows the footsteps of Putin, Russia will be inclined to perpetuate the Bolivarian regimes as well.

**FRANK GAFFNEY:** Great, thank you. I'm glad we got that. In particular, that this infusion of Chinese loans or forward payments for oil may provide some life support that makes Gustavo Coronel's wishful thinking a little bit more wishful. So let's open it up. We don't have microphones, I don't believe. So we would ask you to speak volubly. Identify yourself, please, and your organization, if you have one. And I will try to repeat the question as best I can so that it is picked up by *TeleSUR* and other outlets that are present here today. Ken Timmerman.

*Ken Timmerman asks a question about the utility of a Venezuelan foothold for Iran.*

**FRANK GAFFNEY:** Question is, "How could the Venezuelan base be used for retaliation by Iran?"

**DR. NORMAN BAILEY:** Well, it's not just the Venezuelan base. I would say it's primarily in two areas. One is to interfere with traffic in the Panama Canal. That would actually be remarkably simple to do. I mean, recently, a man was found beheaded in Panama City. It turned out to be one of the divers who attach cylinders of cocaine to the hulls of ships before they go through the canal. Then, at the other end in Rotterdam or wherever the ship is going, they are alerted that there is a cylinder or two in the hull of this particular ship that has taken off at that stage. Well, this diver, it turned out, had stolen fifteen kilos of cocaine from the cylinder and this was the cartel saying, "We don't like that, don't do that." Anyhow, if you can that easily put a cylinder of cocaine on the hull of a ship you can put a cylinder full of high explosives on the hull of a ship also. And then you blow up one or two or three of them in the middle of the canal and you've got a hell of a situation trying to reopen it. The other thing is that the Iranians have mined the oil facilities in Venezuela–the refineries and the pipelines and some of the oil-related port facilities. And this has been done with Iranian technical assistance, and members of the PDVSA workforce–PDVSA is the state oil company of Venezuela–have been trained in how to trigger these devices.

So those are the two principal ways in which the Iranians have arranged to attack the interests of the United States, should they be attacked. And let me just mention, if Israel does the attack, the United States will be blamed for it. Even if Obama goes on worldwide television and says, "Don't do it, don't do it, I hate you Netanyahu," and so on and so forth, the Iranians will say it was done with the support and collaboration of the United States. And they would retaliate against us.

*A male TeleSUR correspondent questions the veracity of alleged connections between the Chavez government and the FARC.*

**FRANK GAFFNEY:** Okay, I heard two questions. One is, "Are there in fact connections between the FARC and the Venezuelan government, or is this really just another house of cards used to justify perhaps military actions against the regime?" Who would like to answer that question? I think we have several takers. Jon.

**JON PERDUE:** For one thing, I would say that if we're going on a standard of preponderance of the evidence, that as more and more Raúl Reyes documents come out from the captured computer, I think the links will be solidified. As far as military action goes, absolutely not. I don't think anybody here is suggesting that. Anything that we would ever do militarily would be strictly retaliatory. The thing I am suggesting, and the only thing I mentioned, was the fact that there are soft measures now that could be taken to thwart or parry these soft subversive efforts that Venezuela is doing now in order to counter them. So you do not ever have to do any kind of military action which would even be retaliatory. Let me see, who else wanted to get in on this?

**GUSTAVO CORONEL:** No, I just want to mention that Venezuela today is a totally militarized country. The popular militia created by Chavez is now in the thousands. I am not saying that they are very efficient, but they are real. So, for all practical purposes, Venezuela is on a war footing. But I don't think and I wouldn't recommend that the United States take any action on Venezuela. My impression is that Chavez is imploding. If the U.S. did not do anything, Chavez would implode. So there is no need for any U.S. invasion.

**FRANK GAFFNEY:** Norm Bailey, I thought you might address yourself to the evidence of the connection between the FARC and the Venezuelan government.

**DR. NORMAN BAILEY:** Well, the evidence is simply overwhelming. I mean, it's like saying that the Holocaust didn't take place or the Armenian massacre in 1915 didn't take place. I mean, when you've got documents, you've got pictures, and you've got everything else. And it was all authenticated by Interpol. I mean, this is disinformation and misinformation carried to the extremes. We can call it "FARC denial" as opposed to Holocaust denial.

**FRANK GAFFNEY:** Among other things, as I recall, there was a certain hard drive that provided very clinical documentation of this connection.

**DR. NORMAN BAILEY:** Absolutely, I mean, the evidence is absolutely overwhelming.

*A woman asks a question about the failed coup attempt against the Chavez regime in 2002.*

**GUSTAVO CORONEL:** Yes. Actually, if you remember April, 2002, and the author of a wonderful book on that event, Brian Nelson, is here with us, Chavez was ousted as a result of a gigantic popular march. And the reluctance of the army to fire on the protesters caused Chavez's ousting. I think this is exactly what is going to happen from here somewhere in time before 2012. The situation in Venezuela is such that there is a very high level of frustration not only among the opposition to Chavez, but even among Chavez's own followers, because as money dwindles, so loyalty dwindles. I mean, the art of keeping everybody happy at the same time is only possible if you have enough money to go around. But Chavez is now getting into great debt. He has quintupled the national debt during his eleven years, and he's now mortgaging the oil of the Orinoco area to the Chinese for a loan of twenty billion dollars. This is illegal. I definitely believe that the popular protests in Venezuela are increasing and will keep increasing up to a point in which the combination of popular protests and the army rejecting Chavez's orders to repress them will result in a new ousting of Chavez, just as it happened April 11th, 2002.

**DR. LUIS FLEISCHMAN:** I just want to disagree with Gustavo on this. I believe that when people say that Chavez's staying in power depends on oil money or on legitimacy they are underestimating the revolutionary mood of Chavez. I think Chavez can stay forever in power for a very long time. Chavez understands that his legitimacy is going to fade away. This is why he is building an alternative totalitarian infrastructure. I think it is wrong for U.S. foreign policy makers to think that Chavez is going to last until he loses his legitimacy or his oil money. I think he can stay for a long time by using plain force. Look at Fidel Castro.

**DR. NORMAN BAILEY:** Yes. One factor that Gustavo didn't mention is that Venezuela now has the highest inflation rate in the Western Hemisphere and one of the highest in the world. That's another effect of the "Bolivarian Revolution." Also, it was not mentioned; when China makes advance payments on delivery of oil, the idea is, "Oh boy, they're going to pay the market prices on it." They don't. That's a myth. In the first place, the Venezuelan mix doesn't get the international price because it's heavy sour crude, by and large. It gets about ten dollars less per barrel than the international price. The international price is about $80 per barrel, while Venezuela gets about $70 per barrel. And the deals that are made by the Chinese are not even at the price for the Venezuelan mix. I don't know about this deal, but in previous deals, it's been about fifteen dollars less than the price. So instead of eighty, it would be seventy, and then it's not seventy, it's fifty-five dollars a barrel. And China has now got a claim on Venezuela's oil production for the rest of time.

**JON PERDUE:** Two quick things for our correspondents from *TeleSUR*. One thing is this increase in Quds Force that are coming from Iran into Venezuela, is a signal of one of two things: either Chavez thinks his support is sinking, or one of his ALBA contemporaries–Evo Morales or Daniel Ortega or Rafael Correa–needs more assistance and training.

But the other thing is there's a case going on right now in Colombia, for instance, of terrorist Jaime Cienfuegos. I've started to get documentation that's coming out of that case that are releases from the Raúl Reyes's documents. These document releases are starting to show all the links between the FARC and everybody else that's been reported previously. Where these documents have been held is classified until now, and we've not been able to see them. But now the links between Chavez and the FARC and others are starting to come out as these caseloads increase and are adjudicated.

**FRANK GAFFNEY:** Are there any questions from people other than Hugo Chavez's information operation? I can see a hand up, but I can't see anybody. Go ahead, stand up, sir, if you would.

*A man asks a question about Panamanian security.*

**DR. NORMAN BAILEY:** Well, first of all, I don't think anybody would ask them if they were going to permit it. Secondly, I do have to say that the new government in Panama is much more security-minded than the previous government and is taking a number of measures to protect the canal during the construction phase for the expansion of the canal, including patrolling the Caribbean side and the Pacific side of Panamanian waters. And it has entrained security systems for the free zone of Colón, which is kind of the tri-border area of North America in terms of nefarious activities, as well as the border between Colombia and Panama, which is almost totally open at this point for the rest and recreation of FARC people, and also the movement of arms and other products back and forth. And as the congresspersons pointed out, we're of course rewarding Panama by refusing to take the free trade agreement to Congress.

*A male questioner notes that Defense Secretary Robert Gates has not publically recognized FARC and Iranian penetration of South America as serious a threat.*

**FRANK GAFFNEY:** Surely, if Robert Gates doesn't see any problem with the FARC or the Iranians, there can't be a problem. Does anybody disagree with that view?

**GUSTAVO CORONEL:** Well, I know about Mr. Gates, of course. I don't know what goes on in the mind of Mr. Gates, but there is plenty of evidence about the links between Hugo Chavez and the FARC. I mean, as Norman says, tons of documents. And in fact I have some videos in my own records.

There is no possibility of denying these links any longer. So I think probably Mr. Gates was just misinformed, but we have to ask him.

**JON PERDUE:** For one thing, this is not too far afield from the past statements of diplomat-speak that have come from either the State Department or the current administration that prefer to use the "benign neglect" strategy. And the other thing is it depends on what the definition of a link is. Maybe if you want to say that Hugo Chavez personally does not have a link to the FARC–or enough of a link to call it a link– then certainly his subordinates do.

**DR. NORMAN BAILEY:** I think it's important to mention that Chavez has admitted he has links to the FARC and supports the FARC. I mean, this is like Adolf Hitler saying, "Yeah, I killed all those six million people," and then saying, "Well, it didn't happen." It's done. It's over. I mean, this is ridiculous, quite frankly.

**FRANK GAFFNEY:** Let me just add my own two bits on this, as the Venezuelan press is having a hard time accepting the evidence here. It's troubling, to say the least, that the United States government is characterizing the relationship between the FARC and the Venezuelan government as it is, and that it is simply choosing to ignore the obvious security implications of having the Iranian regime itself and its surrogates now operating with impunity in our hemisphere. As I said in my opening remarks, I don't consider this benign neglect anymore. This is malign neglect, and people will be killed as a result of it. And I'm afraid that they will not only be people in the parts of this hemisphere south of our border. They will be in this country as well. It is irresponsible not to be looking at this kind of information, this documented information. Some of it is even coming out of the Pentagon itself, for crying out loud. The report that Bill Gertz featured prominently in the *Washington Times* yesterday was drawn from the Pentagon's own report. It is inconceivable to me that the Secretary of Defense could actually be indifferent to the presence of the Quds Force in our hemisphere, which his own department has documented as not only happening, but accelerating.

Any other questions from people other than the Venezuelan press? Yes, ma'am.

*A woman asks a question about the Sao Paulo Forum.*

**FRANK GAFFNEY:** Ah, the Sao Paulo Forum. Why are we not paying attention to this particular threat? Jon.

**JON PERDUE:** There's a book published by Alejandro Peña Esclusa, who has now been arrested by Chavez, about exactly that. But this hasn't been spoken about very much. It's actually a manifesto about exactly everything we're now talking about. It lays out exactly what Hugo Chavez, Fidel Castro, Lula, and the rest of the actors right now are doing. It's a diminution of the military throughout Latin America, etcetera. It is a plan to do this over time–it should be noted that this is a long term plan. And it has been carried out step by step so far. But the meeting of the *Foro de Sao Paulo* that she's talking about–the Sao Paulo Forum, which took place first in 1990.

> **Editor's Note:** *The Foro de Sao Paulo was founded by Fidel Castro and Lula da Silba in response to the fall of the Soviet Union. The first meeting of the Foro took place in 1990, and included leftist and communist parties not only from Latin America, but worldwide. Its mission was to develop a strategy to counter the power and influence of the United States. The Foro is still active, and continues to meet yearly. It includes among its current members and participants several terrorist organizations.*

**JON PERDUE:** And it was just a plan of all the leftist leaders and actually the ex-communist parties or current communist parties in Latin America to get together and to form a strategic plan.

**DR. NORMAN BAILEY:** I wanted to say that Lula and Fidel Castro were two of the main actors in the formation of the *Foro de Sao Paulo*.

**DR. LUIS FLEISCHMAN:** And I would say that Hugo Chavez is using his partners in the *Foro de Sao Paulo* to expand the Bolivarian Revolution, and I think the *Foro de Sao Paulo* was moved to the margins in a way because the Bolivarian Revolution took over.

**DR. NORMAN BAILEY:** They hold a meeting every year.

**DR. LUIS FLEISCHMAN:** Yes, they do. And they have links to Chavez.

**FRANK GAFFNEY:** Could I ask, in this regard, the mention that was made of Lula's external program in contrast to the one he gets such credit for internally? How is he playing the Sao Paulo Forum? And is this, in fact, further evidence of what you've described, Norm, as a very troubling sort of double-game?

**DR. NORMAN BAILEY:** Well, to his credit, he has never pretended to be anything else than a radical when it comes to foreign policy. He isn't saying one thing and doing something else. He attends the meetings every year. He's a great ally of Chavez. Lula's become a best buddy of Ahmadinejad, you know. This isn't anything new. He's been on that side of things since the very beginning. Of course, there's an election later this year, and we can all keep our fingers crossed because if his candidate wins, he will continue to be president of Brazil.

**FRANK GAFFNEY:** The Kirchner model I guess, right? Gustavo.

**GUSTAVO CORONEL:** Just a comment on Ahmadinejad. Lula just visited Iran a few weeks ago, and before he went he said publicly that you have to be very careful with Ahmadinejad because he's a basket case. Now, we have another basket case in Latin America and that's Hugo Chavez. That's why I go and visit with him every three or four months to keep him in check. Can you imagine a president of a Latin American country saying this? And that was in the newspapers in Brazil.

**FRANK GAFFNEY:** Presumably he meant this in the best sense of the word. Whatever that is. Luis.

**DR. LUIS FLEISCHMAN:** I want to say something about the president of Brazil. I don't think he's a Chavista. I think he has moved a little bit into a more pragmatic approach; however, I think he's an enabler. I think it was very irresponsible on the part of Lula de Silva to visit Iran and say that Ahmadinejad has the right to deny the Holocaust. Furthermore, Lula spoke about the right of Iran to have a nuclear weapon. So, I think Lula de Silva, even though domestically he has moved to a more pragmatic side as he included conservatives in his cabinet, I think his policy still pays lip service to the *Foro de Sao Paulo* ideology. I think this is very, very dangerous. Therefore, I agree with Norman. Let's cross our fingers and hope that his party loses the election in October.

**DR. NORMAN BAILEY:** The conservatives in his cabinet were all on the economic side. His foreign minister is extremely leftist; however, to give the devil his due, he did not say that he supports Iran's right to nuclear weapons. He said "yes" to nuclear energy.

**FRANK GAFFNEY:** That's always, of course, the entry point into the nuclear weapons program. Doug Farah, you're going to be speaking momentarily, do you have a quick question?

**DOUGLAS FARAH:** I'll address it there. But I think one of the things with the *Foro de Sao Paulo* is, like Luis said, that the *Coordinadora Continental Bolivariana* has supplanted the *Foro* as something much more FARC-controlled, and much more directly under Chavez's control, and I think he likes that better.

*A man asks whether Venezuela should be recognized as a state sponsor of terrorism and the possibility of imposing sanctions.*

**FRANK GAFFNEY:** Okay. Anybody follow that? This was a very complicated question and, I think, an important question. Norm you addressed yourself to the issue of the implications of Venezuela not being considered a terrorist-sponsoring regime. How might sanctions work, and could this Chinese bailout of Venezuela be applied in the future to Iran as well?

**DR. NORMAN BAILEY:** The premise of the question is not accurate. There have been sanctions applied to Venezuela, particularly financial sanctions, almost entirely by the Treasury Department. Both institutions and individuals have been sanctioned by the Treasury Department. So the premise is not accurate. However, should the U.S. government be doing many other things? Absolutely, and I outlined them in my remarks.

**FRANK GAFFNEY:** But specifically on this question of whether it is a state sponsor of terror, was that not one of your recommendations?

**DR. NORMAN BAILEY:** Yes.

**FRANK GAFFNEY:** Okay. And there's no question in your mind that it qualifies?

**DR. NORMAN BAILEY:** It certainly qualifies. Yes. Absolutely. I said that both times I testified before Engel's subcommittee here in this building.

**FRANK GAFFNEY:** You are nothing if not consistent. Thank you, Norm.

# Panel Two

## CHAVEZ AND THE FARC, MORALES' BOLIVIA, POST-URIBE COLUMBIA, THE MEXICAN NARCO-WAR, AND CONCLUSION

**F**RANK GAFFNEY: He is currently a senior fellow at the International Assessment and Strategy Center. **Douglas Farah** has had a distinguished record in the field of journalism as an investigative reporter and as an author. He will be speaking, especially for those of you who have expressed keen interest in Chavez's connection to the FARC, about how that has manifested itself, particularly in Ecuador and Bolivia. We will then have **Juan Carlos Urenda Diaz**, a Bolivian attorney, offering a firsthand perspective on the Morales government of Bolivia. We will then hear from **Dr. Angel Rabasa**, who's now a senior

*Moderated by* **Frank J. Gaffney, Jr.:** President and Founder, the Center for Security Policy. *This discussion included:* **Douglas Farah:** Senior Fellow, International Assessment and Strategy Center; **Juan Carlos Urenda Diaz:** Bolivian lawyer and author; **Dr. Angel Rabasa:** Senior Policy Analyst, the Rand Corporation; **Ambassador Curtin Winsor:** Former U.S. Ambassador to Costa Rica; and **Ambassador Otto Reich:** Former Assistant Secretary of State for Western Hemisphere Affairs; Former U.S. Ambassador to Venezuela policy analyst at the RAND Corporation. He will be talking about what to anticipate in the post-Uribe environment in Colombia. **Ambassador Curt Winsor**, a good friend of ours here at the Center For Security Policy, former U.S. ambassador to Costa Rica, and a man who has spent most of his life following hemispheric affairs. He will be talking to us about Mexico–both the current situation and I anticipate some forward-looking prognostications, particularly with respect to its implications for America. And the cleanup batter on the second panel will be **Ambassador Otto Reich**. As a former Assistant Secretary of State for Western Hemisphere Affairs he held a senior position with responsibility in this matter. He has also served at least once in the National Security Council and with great distinction as the U.S. ambassador to Venezuela. He will be offering some policy suggestions that flow from all that we have been talking about in the first panel and by his colleagues in the second panel. So with that, Douglas Farah, welcome. We're delighted to have you with us again.

**DOUGLAS FARAH:** Thank you very much. I'm going to talk a little bit about why I think the FARC is still relevant and important, going to the gentleman's question from earlier about why one would believe that there are ties between Mr. Chavez and the FARC. I think if you look at the Reyes documents, which I've had the opportunity to do extensively, everything they say about the relationship between Chavez and the FARC, in Ecuador particularly, has proven now to be true. Particularly in Ecuador, where everyone named in those documents has had to admit that in fact they did deal with the FARC, they interpret it as being a humanitarian effort to lead to the end of the kidnappings, etc.

But I think the strongest indication is, as I mentioned earlier, the *Movimiento Bolivariano Continental*, which was the *Coordinadora Continental Bolivariana*. Earlier this year they formally changed their name in their public meeting in Caracas. One of the group's presidents is always a senior FARC commander. Reyes had been in that position, and the current secretary general of the FARC, Alfonso Cano, currently holds the presidency. They hold open meetings, and they always bring in ETA, they bring in the Irish Republican Army, they bring in Hamas. They bring in other groups that are openly hosted at these forums, and they always proclaim their support for the armed revolution of the FARC. And if you look at the Reyes documents,

*Coordinadora Continental* was founded in 2004 in the Miraflores Palace with FARC funding. And FARC is very upset in some of the documents. They write back and forth with Chavez and others that they're not getting due recognition for the formation of the *Coordinadora Continental*. They are upset that people don't know that it's them. So I think there's significant evidence there.

Over the past couple of years, the Colombian government and military have given priority to clearing out the center of the country, and, as they've done that, they've pushed the FARC consistently to the border regions. And that's why you see the change in the role of Ecuador as it has morphed from its traditional relationship of simply being a rear guard area, where the FARC can come and go and buy medicine and do certain things in a relatively benign way, to Ecuador becoming a vital operational center for the FARC. They need it now to survive. And I think you see the same thing on the Venezuelan side of the Columbian border, because they now need those border regions in ways that they didn't need them before. At the International Assessment and Strategy Center, we just did a very long paper on Ecuador and its ties to the FARC. I brought a few copies up there on the table, which you're welcome to. It's also online at www.strategycenter.net, and it goes into great detail on the FARC presence in the Ecuadorian political system, the Ecuadorian process, and the importance of Ecuador. I just want to highlight a couple of things in this regard. The FARC has calculated correctly that, after the Angostura bombing that killed Raúl Reyes on March 1, 2008, Colombia could not pay the political cost of going into Ecuador again. And so the FARC simply has moved itself, lock, stock, and barrel, across the border into Ecuador, because they actually feel safer there now than they did in the prior situation. And so you now see for the first time large HCL labs–the stuff you stick up your nose, hydrochloride cocaine–in Ecuador as opposed to in Colombia. And the other dynamic that's underway is there are no longer major cartels in Colombia that can broker international deals.

The FARC now produces about 70-75% percent of the HCL product, but they don't have an international trafficking structure to move that out to the international market. And what you see now is the Mexican organizations arriving in Ecuador to buy the HCL product and shipping it north– putting it on their semi-submersibles, or their aircraft, or their go-fast boats, or their tuna boats, and all the different methods they use. But this is facilitated greatly by two things. First, the Correa government's tolerance, if not embracing of the FARC–at least some very senior individuals in the Correa government. Second is the fact that Ecuador, through its economic crisis in 2000, "dollarized" its economy. So what you have now–and I was at Lago Agrio and spent a lot of time on the border there fairly recently–is that the Mexicans are coming in with dollars that they get from the cocaine. They can deposit it into bank accounts in Ecuador that are controlled by the FARC, and the FARC can simply use an ATM card to withdraw the cash they need. It's a much easier process than it used to be where you had to convert the money into pesos and bring it back over, and it was much more bulky and much more difficult to do. Now you have a dollar to dollar transaction. And what's really frightening to the people on the borders is that you now have groups of Mexicans coming in, and particular middle men are embedded with the FARC, Mexican middle men, who have their own security apparatuses or own people that they bring with them. They're treated as senior FARC combatants would be, and they deal directly with the FARC commanders. This process is not an exceptionally new one; it's just accelerated greatly over the past several years, particularly with the 48th front of the FARC, which does the cocaine trafficking for them, and the 29th front, which handles the weapon shipments. And so you have this criminalization of the border regions, certainly in Anap. They actually did a commission to investigate the Angostura bombing where Raúl Reyes was killed, and the gist of it was that a very respected academic was appointed by Correa, a friend of Correa's who was supposed to come out and say it was all an American plot and a horrible thing. And he did do some of that, but he actually dug into the case rather deeply and came out and wrote an extensive document, a hundred and seventy pages, saying, "My God, we've become a narco-state, and look what's happened to us." And he was concerned enough about whether Correa would allow the paper to be published to give a series of interviews prior to publication to make sure the information was out there. The report did come out, and now it's available online. It's a really interesting internal look from an honest academic close to Correa, looking at the situation of his country and essentially saying, "We're really screwed." So I think that that's incredibly important.

A third factor that comes in with this is that Ecuador has lifted all its visa restrictions on virtually everyone in the world. So what you're seeing is a huge influx of Russian organized crime and Chinese organized crime and other organized crime groups, because, like water running downhill, they'll go to the place where it's easiest to operate. And unfortunately for Ecuador, that right now is Ecuador. So you see this sort of shift over there where it's much more complex for the Ecuadorians to manage. The Ecuadorians argue, and rightly so, that it is not their war. And it is not a war that they want a part of. And if they actually began to take on the FARC in serious military ways, the FARC could very easily blow up their oil infrastructure and they would be in very deep trouble.

The FARC provides us with, in its own words and in its own videos, ample evidence of many things. And when Correa was elected, they write a letter, a congratulatory letter, saying, "Oh my God, this is great. We're very happy that you were elected." They write to several of his senior officials to congratulate them and say, "We're so glad you're there and we look forward to working with you." And along the border region they begin registering Colombian FARC supporters as Ecuadorians to vote in the elections on behalf of Correa–something that's been amply documented in the Angostura report and in other things.

Finally, I think one of the things that we don't look at seriously, and it goes a little bit to what Norman and others were saying earlier, is this particular book, which is called *La Guerra Periferica y el Islamic Revolucionario* or *Peripheral Warfare and Radical Islam: Origins, Rules and Ethics in Asymmetrical Warfare*. It wouldn't have been a very important book. It was written by a Spanish academic named Jorge Verstrynge. Essentially, the thesis of the book is that Osama bin Laden and Carlos the Jackal have showed us the way to defeat the "empire." That we can move forward and–because if we take away all the preconceived notions we had about killing civilians–we can use biological weapons, use nuclear weapons, and we can defeat the "empire"– the "empire" being the United States. And this would have been a very unknown and miserable little book on its own, except that President Chavez got a hold of it, invited the author to give the keynote address at the Asymmetrical Warfare Conference in 2005, and has adopted this as Venezuelan military theory. He had pocket-sized editions of this book printed up and given to every officer in his corps–I can show you the pocket-sized version–with orders to study it and really immerse themselves in this type of military theory. The person who wrote it is neither Muslim nor a military man, but his thesis is that "the South" has to ally itself together against "the empire" and defeat it, and this is the way to do it. And just to finish, if you look around the world at the only group capable of doing the type of warfare that this gentleman describes, it is Hezbollah. And if you look at the relationship between Chavez and the FARC, Iran and Hezbollah, it's not hard to see where part of that relationship is going. I'll leave it there.

**FRANK GAFFNEY:** Terrific, Doug. Thank you so much. Next we have Juan Carlos Urenda Diaz with his perspective from Bolivia. Welcome.

**JUAN CARLOS URENDA DIAZ:** Thank you very much. I'm going to talk about why the Evo Morales regime is a threat to continental security. I'm going to talk about several points.

The first one is an increase in the production of cocaine in Bolivia. Ever since Evo Morales, who holds two public posts–the president of the republic and the president of the six unions of coca producers–became president of the country, coca and cocaine production has surged by three hundred percent. The cocaine flows through Brazil and Argentina, with Europe being its final destination. A large percentage of this may also be entering the U.S. Bolivia allows for a maximum of twelve thousand hectares of coca crops to be grown for traditional uses and consumption. But under the current government there are now over thirty thousand hectares being grown according to a United Nations report.

Second point is the relations with Iran and the potential supply of uranium. Bolivia never traditionally maintained relations with Iran, but under the Evo Morales regime and Hugo Chavez it has become an important ally to our country. The president of the country has publicly supported the nuclear program of Iran. Therefore, since Bolivia has significant reserves of uranium, lithium, and other minerals, Bolivia is likely to supply uranium to Iran. As a matter of fact, the governor of Potosi–one of the provinces of Bolivia–has acknowledged that exploration of uranium is already in place.

Also, on April 2, in Caracas, Venezuela, Morales participated in a ceremony with Chavez and Putin where Venezuela signed an agreement with Russia for the purchase of weapons. Bolivia also made a commitment to purchase one hundred and fifty million dollars in weapons. Russia has also offered Evo Morales' government help in building a nuclear energy plant and the provision of missiles.

In addition, the U.S. ambassador and other U.S agencies have been expelled from the country. As you know, on September 10th, 2008, president Evo Morales expelled the U.S. ambassador in Bolivia Philip Goldberg. Shortly afterwards he also expelled the Drug Enforcement Agency (DEA) and the United States Agency for International Development (USAID). The country is now left exposed to drug trafficking. Now there is no international control over the drug trafficking that goes on inside Bolivia.

In Bolivia, there are also violations of human rights. This is very important because these types of violations might be imitated by other countries on the continent. From the government in public statements and with the full knowledge of the president of the republic, acts of state abuse, such as massacres, are being committed frequently. Such acts have been carried out by police and military forces in the city of Sucre in November of 2007. In another case, three foreigners were executed in the Las Americas Hotel by elite police forces under explicit orders from Evo Morales. The government is also purging the opposition in the department of Santa Cruz.

Criminalization of political activities is also common. These persecutions are carried out by manipulating the courts and the public prosecutors' offices in open violation of the principles of due process and natural jurisdiction. Likewise, testimonies are being obtained by means of torture. The governments of Hungary, Ireland, and Croatia have demanded an international investigation in the case of the three foreigners who were nationals of the countries mentioned above, but such demands are going nowhere because the orders were given by Evo Morales.

There are clear signals of destruction of democratic principles. The division of powers has disappeared. Evo Morales controls the judicial, legislative, and executive branches. About ten days ago, the legislative branch gave Evo Morales the full power to appoint, at his pleasure, all the members of the Supreme Court and the Constitutional Court. Anyone who does not follow his orders is susceptible to lawsuits. The government also encourages "community justice"–violent attacks against individuals initiated by the community–which is used to purge the opposition. That happened with the indigenous leader Marcial Fabricano and former vice president of the republic Victor Hugo Cardenas. These forms of political violence are justified by the government based on the new constitution and approved illegally. The constitution contains racist clauses that violate the principle of equality of all the citizens under the law.

I have brought with me a dossier that will sustain all that I have mentioned here. I have also brought a paper written by myself in English that is called "The State of Catoblepas." Catoblepas is a monster that devours itself–a mythical monster. This is how I describe a critical aspect of this new constitution that is basically racist and also destroys the principles of liberal democracy. This is quite important, because this is probably the blueprint of this 21st century socialism that is following the lead of the Chavez regime. This is also important because the rest of the countries of the continent, especially in South America and Central America, may look at this process and may follow this regime, this path.

Basically, this 21st century socialist regime is being elected through votes and then once in power it turns into an autocratic regime. Evo Morales has modified the constitution to legalize his continuing reelection. There are signals that he may be again calling for a vote, for a plebiscite, to secure another term. So I will provide Nancy Menges a dossier of the documentation that sustains what I have mentioned. This dossier is written in Spanish and in English and provides an account of the new Bolivian constitution. Thank you very much.

**FRANK GAFFNEY:** Juan Carlos, thank you. An important assessment of yet another of the places where this sort of Chavista playbook is rolling out. Next up, we have Dr. Angel Rabasa from RAND speaking about Colombia–the post-Uribe Colombia. Welcome.

**DR. ANGEL RABASA:** First, I would like to thank Frank Gaffney and Nancy Menges for organizing this important event, and I am particularly pleased that you have given me the opportunity to talk about Colombia. Over the last ten years, since the inauguration of Plan Colombia in 2000, Colombia has been a model for counter-insurgency and for U.S. assistance to a government fighting an insurgency. And if one goes back to the mid-1990s, one can see how dramatic the change has been in the situation of Colombia.

In the mid-90's, it looked as if the Revolutionary Armed Forces of Colombia (FARC) was about to take over parts of the country. The FARC, in fact, was able to defeat battalion-size units of the Colombian Army in combat. U.S. assistance was completely focused on counter-narcotics. So if a FARC unit was attacking a town, a police station, or a military unit, the Colombians could not use helicopters provided by the United States unless there was a counter-narcotics interest involved.

That situation actually began to change before the inauguration of President Alvaro Uribe when General Tapias, the commander of the Colombian Armed Forces, began to develop a more effective counter-insurgency approach. But it was President Uribe who really changed the Colombian strategy, and he did it by implementing classical counterinsurgency doctrine. That is to say, by focusing on the consolidation of control of territory and protection of the population. And I think that Colombia has much to teach the United States at a time when we are engaged in a difficult counterinsurgency campaign in Afghanistan.

During his first term, Uribe increased defense spending by thirty percent. He imposed a special tax to support the counterinsurgency efforts. He expanded the size of the security forces by eighty thousand between 2001 and 2004, and began to involve the population in the counterinsurgency. His government established a police presence in every one of Colombia's *municipios*, or territorial jurisdictions. Previously, about a third of them had no police presence, which meant that the FARC could go in at any time and take effective control.

But I don't have enough time to go into all that has been accomplished in Colombia. I just want to focus on some things that are not very well-known in the United States but that were very significant for the success of the Colombian counter-insurgency effort. One was that the Colombians were able to align operations with intelligence, and this is a very difficult thing that took the Colombians years to accomplish with U.S. support. And what happens now is that the Colombians have established dedicated military units to pursue particular high-value targets, such as senior FARC leaders. Once the location of these individuals is determined through technical and human intelligence sources, the Colombians can coordinate air strikes within twenty-four hours. And this has been very successful in decapitating the FARC in many regions of Colombia.

Another very important accomplishment is that Colombia is now moving from counterinsurgency to what one could call the "post-counterinsurgency" phase. There is a growing conviction in Colombia that the FARC has been strategically defeated, that it has been driven out of strategic parts of the country into the frontiers. Of course, they should not be counted out yet. I will mention some very significant challenges that the next Colombian government is going to face. Because, even though the FARC has been broken in the sense that the central FARC leadership no longer has command and control over units, as shown in Operation Check, and the rescue of Ingrid Betancourt and the other hostages, there is still the problem of FARC sanctuaries in Venezuela.

Nevertheless, the challenge for Colombia is not so much to deal with the remnants of the FARC but to bring the state to areas of Colombia that had never had a state presence in the past. The last time I visited Colombia in March 2009, I was flown by helicopter to the town of Chengue in a region on the Caribbean coast called Montes de Maria, which had been the stronghold of FARC warlord Martin Caballero. Chengue was the scene of a massacre some years ago and the population had fled. Now they are beginning to go back. There are Colombian Marines stationed in the town helping the locals resume some level of normality. They have arranged with supermarkets in Bogota to purchase the local produce. This is what they are doing at the local level, reconstructing the country.

And to do that, the Colombian government established a very sophisticated mechanism called the Center for Coordinated Integrated Action at the presidential level. This center is supposed to coordinate the efforts of all of the ministries and government agencies in order to produce an integrated state response to the challenges of reconstruction. We can learn from the Colombians as we try to help build institutions in Afghanistan.

Now, what are the challenges? The challenges are the following. First of all, the levels of U.S. assistance to Colombia are coming down dramatically. The United States and Colombia are engaged in what has been called the "Colombianization" or nationalization of U.S. assets in Colombia. The Colombians believe that they can fill this gap with their own resources;

however, there are going to be critical gaps that will be very difficult for the Colombians to fill–for example, the maintenance of air mobility assets. So it's incumbent now on the United States government to direct whatever aid that the United States can provide to those critical needs of the Colombians.

The second challenge is to continue the process of consolidating a state presence in areas recovered from insurgents, criminals and other anti-social elements. Again, it will be difficult for the Colombian government to extend this effort throughout the country. There will be need for assistance, and in this regard USAID's Office of Transition Initiatives (OTI) has provided some very important support that should be continued.

But the major challenge is that history shows that insurgencies can be very difficult to defeat if they have sanctuaries across the border in other countries. So the Colombians are very concerned about the behavior of neighboring states. But as was mentioned by Douglas Farah, the FARC has moved lock, stock, and barrel into the Venezuelan side of the border, and that includes the entire Caribbean Bloc of the FARC. So now there is a situation where the FARC is waiting for opportunities on the Venezuelan side of the border.

Venezuelan President Chavez has been purchasing large quantities of Russian arms. There is a possibility that if the domestic situation in Venezuela deteriorates, he may rely on an external adventure. The Venezuelan government is already waging asymmetrical warfare against Colombia and against Peru as well, using the *Casas del ALBA* and other "friendship houses" established by the Venezuelan and Cuban governments, as was documented by an investigating committee of the Peruvian Congress. But Colombia is particularly susceptible to this type of threat. In conclusion, the Colombians have achieved enormous successes in their counter-insurgency campaign, but the challenges that lay ahead are quite serious and will require continued U.S. support.

**FRANK GAFFNEY:** Wonderful. Angel, thank you. We turn next to Ambassador Curt Winsor to talk about the most immediate of the hemispheric challenges to this country, namely our neighbor to the immediate south, Mexico. Ambassador Winsor, welcome.

**AMB. CURT WINSOR:** Thank you very much, Frank. I am delighted to have this opportunity to share my concerns with this audience about what is happening to the immediate south of the United States. My colleague just described the successes of the Colombians against the FARC and, to some extent, against the Colombian drug cartels. These developments have pushed the location of a major part of the struggle with the massive corrupting and murderous activities of the big narcotics traffickers from Colombia to Mexico.

I would like to talk about the nature and effects of this growing struggle in Mexico. I would also like to talk about the extent to which Mexico is a "tip point" for significant U.S. national security interests–because of its proximity, because of the enormity of the narco-trafficking, because of illegal immigration and because of Islamist security problems associated with our sporadically defended Mexican border.

Mexico's present struggles and challenges are very much akin to those that confronted Colombia seven to eight years ago when their cartels were battling for position. The Colombian government was struggling with both the Medellin and Cali cartels and the FARC, a terrorist guerrilla force. In the case of Mexico, there is no guerrilla war as of the present; however, the problems that have been created by the cartels are immediate and have become very serious to the survival of government in Mexico.

The Mérida Conference supposedly offered U.S. assistance to Mexico for dealing with the narco-struggle. Evidence, or lack thereof, suggests that very little useful American assistance has materialized from this event beyond some understandings about U.S. interests in counter-narcotics and limited amounts of equipment that mirrored the Colombian conflict, but it is less germane to the needs of the Mexicans.

Mexico's interest in counter-narcotics struggle and warfare is mixed. If you're a Rolex dealer, if you are a real estate dealer, if you are a banker, what's going on in Mexico right now is expanding some of your markets. And if you're wealthy, you can buy security. You can buy an armored car. You don't yet have to use a helicopter as they do in Sao Paulo because of endemic violence, but you can get along. This is not so for Mexico's less wealthy people. They get caught in the crossfire. Their streets are dangerous places because of unrestrained use of automatic weapons by narcos, usually against each other. Businesses are forced to close as the narco "soldiers" set up protection rackets or resort to straight out robbery.

The unrestrained warfare among the narco cartels within Mexico is increasing. The scope of the struggle has stymied Mexican government efforts to directly confront the fevered combatants. The government's objective is not so much to shut down the flow of illegal substances. Mexico's president might well wish to do so, but these huge revenue sources bring significant amounts of money that in very complex ways benefit the economy of Mexico. However, the threat of the power of the cartels against law and order in the country has forced the government to put its major efforts into dividing, splintering, and dealing with the cartels militarily to keep them from uniting and becoming an overwhelming force.

This apparent strategy is not something we hear much about up here. This is because many of us are not aware of how complex and how dynamic the cartel battles and differentiations are within Mexico. Their strength is such that the Mexican government's principal tactic in its struggles with the cartels today is not to defeat them but to keep them off balance. The government of Mexico has been attempting to achieve a kind of equilibrium between the warring cartels that would reduce violence and, though this will never be said publicly, make sure that Mexico benefits in some way from the huge cash flows that are coming into the cartels, much of which sticks to Mexico. The Mexican government has actually intervened to favor certain cartels over others in specific instances.

The early stage of inter-cartel violence in Mexico had local cartels muscling out Colombian cartels. There was and is so much money involved in the illegal commodities trade that the Mexicans felt that they did not need the original Colombian cartels. Today, elements within the Mexican cartels feel that they don't need the original Mexican cartels or their leaders either, so the splintering and the disequilibrium that has occurred has complicated the government's own divisive strategy. The government's divisive approach worked best when there were larger and fewer cartels. So the government is struggling and, some say, even favoring one of the Mexican cartels in order to have less violence and to have a balance of power among the ever-changing cast of narco-players. This has become an enormously complicated situation.

Today in Mexico, the Calderon government is receiving serious blowback from the violence that is affecting all but the very wealthy people of Mexico. You don't hear about the rich families having security problems unless they're "narco-rich." The "narco-rich" families are in wars, so you do indeed see the battles and the casualty lists from them. You see serious and even tragic casualties from the local governments and the federal government elements fighting the more direct and visible battles with the excesses of the cartels, but you do not see such discomfort for much of the Mexican elite.

The loss of safety and stability due to narco-conflicts has almost destroyed important traditional components of the Mexican economy. Tourism is down. The manufacturing sector is depressed for two reasons. New companies do not want to take the risk of violence that would be associated with coming into Mexico. Small businesses, which traditionally have been very important in Mexico, have been victims of extortion arising from the breakdown of law and order in key areas of the country. Small businessmen are preyed upon through protection rackets or outright robbery by the cartel's warrior thugs as a sidebar. By any reckoning, this constitutes an economic dislocation and is taking an immense human toll on the majority of Mexicans.

Finally, and very importantly, we are seeing an upsurge in political fear and a resulting pressure on the Calderon government from people who are being forced to take extraordinary measures to defend themselves. They look to the government whose narrow victory some years back was based on their plan to be able to reduce the violence. They've tried to do it again, but for various reasons they're not succeeding.

If I've created a complex picture, that is my intention. The situation in Mexico is dangerously complex. Yet the growing crisis in Mexico is one in which the United States government is not playing an effective role. This is because we look at Mexico as we look at Colombia and as we look at other areas of the hemisphere with not benign, but malign neglect.

Latin America is simply at the bottom of the totem pole of U.S. interests today. The reason we're not paying more attention to what's happening in Venezuela or to Iranian adventures in the region is that we are distracted. I would say we are putting more of our national security interests right now in Africa than we are Latin America.

Since the end of the Reagan administration, Latin American assistant secretaries of state have in effect been denied the attention that the region deserves within the policy levels of the U.S. government, and that puts them at a tremendous disadvantage. Such neglect allows the counter-narcotics issue alone to drive our national security perceptions for the region, and this is courting disaster. It is at the very least irresponsible to reduce our attention, our aid, and our dwindling influence in the region to anti-narcotics efforts.

I would like to at least mention several other concerns about Mexico that aren't widely noticed in the United States, given the narco-driven violence and convulsions that we have just discussed. But we have been ignoring fundamental issues within Mexico that are quite apart from the destabilizing effects of the narco-struggle. My friend, Roger Pardo Maurer, has written an excellent paper on this area, which is beginning to get attention. He raises seven questions–none of which we think about much up here but which will immensely affect Mexico. And in terms of the U.S. border, they will eventually affect the United States.

One of Mexico's critical problems is the scarcity and misallocation of water. Mexico is not allocating its water wisely. There are water shortages that are already beginning to manifest from the needs of cities that are not getting it. Water coming to Mexico from across the border in the United States is becoming a problem because we're still using the wasteful practice of flood irrigation in southern California to raise alfalfa. Water is a major problem for the future of Mexico, just as it is for China, the western United States, and a number of other countries in the future.

The falling production of Mexico's oil fields is a major problem, including loss of revenues. Mexico's corrupt petroleum union leadership and various other factors have led to the neglect, lack of maintenance, and lack of improvement or expansion of their oil fields. Mexican oil production is declining precipitously. It is said to have declined as much as fourteen percent in the past year.

Industrial competitiveness has become a new problem for Mexico. Ross Perot's reference to the "great sucking sound" of U.S. jobs going to Mexico from NAFTA during the campaign of 1992 is not evident. Today, it's not jobs going out of the United States to Mexico, but Mexican jobs that are going to China or have already gone to China.

Mexican regionalism has become an issue. There exist serious problems in the south of Mexico *vis-a-vis* other areas. Among these factors are poverty and the status of indigenous peoples who have not benefitted from education or economic opportunity.

Mexico even has demographic problems. Numbers of young Mexicans immigrate legally and illegally to the United States. But they have no place to return to in Mexico. This is going to create tremendous instabilities within Mexico itself. The exportation of Mexico's underemployed young people is no longer a long-term option that Mexico can afford. Future scenarios suggest shortages of manpower for Mexico within twenty years if present trends continue.

I would like to wrap up my talk today with a strong recommendation toward resolving the narco-violence problems of Mexico and of the United States. I believe the only way we can help Mexico in its present violent convulsion, as well as related issues in Bolivia, Colombia, and Ecuador, is for the United States to legalize certain criminalized substances. I would include marijuana on this list.

Although pot is no longer the principle product of the cartels, it is an immensely profitable and high volume product. Cocaine powder itself should also be legalized. Not crack, which is swiftly and violently addictive, but powder cocaine itself. The legalization of these commodities would curtail the two highest volume and profitable commodities that feed the narco-cartels. This is a "war" that can be fought with market mechanisms. Lower prices for pot and cocaine would restrict what is now an unencumbered flood of disruptive money from the U.S. into the cartels.

We are surely aware that we have not been able to interfere with the market mechanisms for demand of these products in the U.S. The analogy with the failure of the prohibition of alcohol is evident. However, we can engage with favorable mechanisms in Mexico and in the U.S. by radically reducing the wild profitability upon which the narcos feed and destabilize Latin America and other areas of the world. Legalization of these commodities could be the less onerous way in which the United States could both help itself and its neighbors from an international problem that has negative social, political, and economic consequences for us and most certainly for our neighbors to the south.

My second point, which is off my main topic but germane to the discussion today, would be that the United States should find petroleum from areas other than Venezuela, even from our own stockpile if necessary. Today, Hugo Chavez is critically dependent upon U.S. markets for the vast majority of his oil exports. This will not always be the case, but by cutting our purchases of his highly acidic and sulphur-rich oil, we would precipitate a fatal crisis for his regime, which has limited storage facilities for unsold oil. This also would productively use market mechanisms and bring down a sworn enemy in a way that would be nonviolent. Thank you.

**FRANK GAFFNEY:** Ambassador Winsor, thank you very much, particularly for that quite provocative first recommendation. You introduced perfectly our wrap-up speaker, one of the assistant secretaries of state who had access but not always the attention of his superiors, despite valiant efforts and certainly a compelling case. Welcome, Otto Reich. Thank you for joining us and for hopefully giving us some other recommendations, perhaps provocative as well.

**OTTO REICH:** Thank you very much, Frank, and let me thank Nancy also for organizing this event. I'm impressed by the way that everybody stuck to their ten or twelve minutes, and I will try to do the same.

I've been asked to wrap up and provide some policy recommendations. I think wrapping up is relatively easy. What the United States is confronting in the hemisphere today is a major challenge to our security. It is a challenge from an alliance called ALBA, the Spanish acronym for the "Bolivarian Alternative of the Americas," that was created in Havana. It is not new. It is only the latest iteration of an effort that Fidel Castro created in the 1960's. At that time he called it "Tri-Continental" where he joined together radical, anti-American, terrorist, and any other groups from three continents that would follow his view of a hemisphere free of the United States.

Today that effort is being financed primarily by Venezuela through Hugo Chavez. So it was created in Havana, but it's being funded by Venezuelan oil. It's a snake whose tail reaches all the way down to Bolivia, through Nicaragua, through Ecuador, and has gotten into places like Honduras where it was expelled constitutionally–expelled by a Honduran population that learned the separation of powers and did not fall for the mistaken prescriptions of the current U.S. administration.

I really don't know what's happening to the U.S. government today. We are making a lot of mistakes. The first mistake is that we're not recognizing the challenge that we're facing in the hemisphere. The fact is that there is this ALBA alliance of eight countries, including three small Caribbean countries which I never really mention. I don't want to pick on them because they are so poor and small that when Hugo Chavez comes around with bags of money, as he does, and bribes people with enormous amounts of money, it's very hard for the leaders of a country of a hundred thousand people and no resources to turn him down.

But some of the other countries are much more dangerous. And the United States must have the political will to recognize the aggression that is taking place. The aggression is not the same aggression of the Cold War that can be countered with missiles and conventional weapons. We are being undermined–our interests are being undermined–by subversion. Earlier, we talked about the FARC, the Revolutionary Armed Forces of Colombia, which is a Marxist army that has been designated as a terrorist organization by the U.S., the EU and others. We haven't even mentioned some of the other groups that are being funded by Chavez and by ALBA. We know that Mr. Chavez has surreptitiously funded many electoral campaigns in this hemisphere. We know, for example, that he gave millions of dollars to Cristina Kirchner, the current president of Argentina, who was here in Washington not too long ago and was received as if she were just another politician who had won a fair campaign. We know she received money from Chavez only because two years ago there was a trial in U.S. Federal Court in Miami that clearly demonstrated that the Kirchner government received at least eight hundred thousand dollars from Chavez. That was actually one shipment of what was a four million dollar contribution. Such contributions are illegal under Argentine law and even illegal under Venezuelan law, and that's why it was done surreptitiously.

The same kind of surreptitious contributions have been made in Ecuador, Peru, Bolivia, Nicaragua, and other countries. I have spoken to businessmen who told me they had been ordered to take money to some of those countries, in cash, for the campaigns of people who are today in power in some of those countries. Some of those campaigns failed, like in Panama. There's no question that the losing candidate in Panama received money from Chavez. In El Salvador the winning party, the FMLN, did receive money from Chavez illegally and surreptitiously.

There are a number of ways that we're being challenged: the military buildup in Venezuela is one, financed by the Soviet Union, sorry, Freudian slip, by Russia; by Iran, the connections with Iran, which we talked about here today; and the connections with radical Arab groups, like Hezbollah. Frank mentioned that the *Washington Times* talked about a Pentagon report about Iranian Special Forces, the Quds Forces, being present in Venezuela. If this is not a direct challenge to the United States, then what is? Well, what is our government doing about it? Frankly, what our government is trying to do at the moment is they're still reaching out.

What president Obama said in his inaugural address about reaching out to those who are oppressing their peoples is still happening. And, by the way, every one of these countries is oppressing their people. These governments of ALBA are oppressors. They have no freedom of the press. I understand, for example, that *TeleSUR*, which is an organ of the Venezuelan government, is here today. I wish that they would ask their owner, Hugo Chavez, to have freedom of the press in Venezuela so that when people speak out in Venezuela they are not thrown in jail. Gustavo Alvarez Paz, a former member of congress and a very respected, peaceful person who had never been accused of any crime, was thrown in jail for saying exactly what everybody in the world is saying about what is taking place in Venezuela.

So Chavez is funding these aggressors who are also oppressors. What should the United States do? People say, "Oh, there's nothing we can do about Chavez." That is completely false. There are three things that can be done right now that do not require any legislation. They have been recommended by the staff of the National Security Council and others. I know because I was one of those who recommended some of them, and, frankly, I didn't win the argument at that time.

At some point, I think these things will be done. Just like the United States in 1941 refused to declare an embargo on oil and scrap iron against the Japanese until it was too late, I think the United States should do three things about Venezuela right now. Venezuela is the head of the snake. The brain is in Havana, but the head is in Caracas.

First, declare Venezuela to be a state sponsor of terrorism. The evidence is there. The State Department has it. The Defense Department has it. The Congress has it. The political will is missing. Second, revoke the visas of Chavez's business allies, his business partners, and what the Venezuelans call *"Boliburgeses"* or "Bolivarian bourgeoisie." By being Chavez's business partners, they have become multimillionaires and, in many cases, billionaires who own homes in the United States and travel back and forth to Venezuela. They are the ones who carry those bags full of money to Daniel Ortega in Nicaragua, Ollanta Humala in Peru, Evo Morales in Bolivia when he was running for office, or to Christina Kirchner in Argentina. By the way, the party of the current president of Brazil, Lula da Silva's party, also received money from Venezuela. It's been reported in the Brazilian press. So this subversion of the institutions of democracy is taking place under our noses, and the United States is saying nothing.

This is happening today in Nicaragua. Daniel Ortega is again trying to subvert the democratic institutions that brought him to office, and I have not seen a single protest from the State Department. The *Washington Post* has an editorial today about it. I hope the State Department will have the backbone to say something, to speak up for democracy in Nicaragua as it pretended to speak up for democracy in Honduras but made a terrible mistake—a policy mistake that Secretary Clinton had to reverse. That's another story. I hope we have some time to talk about what happened in Honduras because it was a colossal mistake by this administration; it was such a mistake of judgment or intelligence or intention that it has to be examined. Because if we continue with that kind of attitude, we're going to undermine our own interests.

The third policy prescription I suggest, a simple nonviolent policy pre-scription, is for the United States to announce that it is ending its dependence on Venezuelan oil. Some people say, "Oh, we can't do this," and I reply, "Of course we can do this." We import six percent of our consumption from Ven-ezuela. Two years ago when the price of oil hit a hundred and forty dollars a barrel, the American people, because of the magic of the marketplace, reduced our consumption of oil by eight percent, because the price of gasoline was too high. So we reduced our consumption in one year by more than we import from Venezuela in an entire year. Of course we can replace Venezuela.

Second, four hundred thousand barrels of the little over a million that we import from Venezuela can only be refined in specially designed refiner-ies in the United States. By the way, it used to be a million and a half barrels a day. Chavez would have to absorb the four hundred thousand barrels of heavy crude if the United States said, "No more crude from Venezuela."

And that is another point: Venezuela has a maximum of ten days' storage for all of its production of oil. If the United States were to say, "No more oil from Venezuela," in ten days they'd have to shut down the fields. It would cause such an economic crisis for Venezuela that the Venezuelans would have to question the sanity of the man in power in Caracas. What they do about it, that's their decision, but the United States should be defending its own interests. Those are the three quick recommendations. There are a lot of others but I'm getting the hook, so I want to leave plenty of time for questions and maybe some comments from the audience. Thank you.

*A question is asked about irregular wafare.*

**AMB. CURT WINSOR:** I don't think irregular warfare is the principal threat in Latin America. It is a threat in Colombia and perhaps Peru, but in most of Latin America we don't have irregular warfare—we have political corruption. It's something we've seen before and we'll see again, and it can be dealt with. We are not choosing to deal with it these days because we're not paying attention to the region.

I think the principal issue is that we have to get our thinking beyond counter-narcotics. But that in turn is going to force us to come to the conclusion that we're going to have to be reengaged in the hemisphere. Somebody said basically that the objective of Hugo Chavez and Fidel Castro was to have the United States disappear from the hemisphere. Well, in part, they have succeeded. We have pretty much retreated from active engagement in and with the hemisphere. And the fact that we are attempting to spend hundreds of millions of dollars of the taxpayer's money on alternative crops to cocaine when there's no market, transportation, or infrastructure for those crops demonstrates the futility of what we are about.

**FRANK GAFFNEY:** Can I ask a sort of a refinement to this? It seems to me maybe irregular warfare is less an issue than asymmetric warfare, and we talked a little bit about that in the previous panel. But could somebody speak to the perceived if not actual role of President Obama himself and his seeming affinity for Hugo Chavez—perhaps not the Chavez agenda, but Chavez the man—in multilateral fora and within the hemisphere? Otto, do you want to speak to that?

**OTTO REICH:** You know, I think one of the problems with this president is we still don't know exactly who he is and what his real intentions are. There's no question that, for example, a year ago when he went to Trinidad and Tobago for the Summit of the Americas, in my view, and I wrote at the time, he made a mistake with his warm embrace of Hugo Chavez. A handshake is sort of required at these diplomatic meetings, but not the slap on the back and the big smile and all the conversations. People–especially our adversaries– see that kind of gentility as weakness. They don't see it as courtesy. In fact, the next day, we saw that Chavez had figured, "Oh, you know, I can handle this guy." And he gave President Obama an anti-American, anti-European book that, frankly, lies about history. Giving Obama this book was in itself an act of propaganda; it is a book that says that all the problems of Latin America are the fault of the United States and Europe. And this book was in Spanish. The president doesn't speak Spanish, so he didn't know–he couldn't know–what he was getting. But he put himself in that situation.

That's one example. You could ascribe that to lack of experience, naiveté, or being a rookie on the world stage. But how do you explain that when El Salvador has a presidential election where one of the two parties who are running head to head was the FMLN party, the party of the guerillas that had killed not only Salvadorians but American citizens, and several members of this Congress go to El Salvador and say–as they did also in Washington–that the Salvadorian people in their sovereign use of their ballot should be careful not to elect a government that could undermine democracy in El Salvador. And everybody knew who they were talking about: it was that the American Embassy and the State Department said that we were neutral in that election. How can we be neutral in an election where one of the parties has as a vice-presidential candidate who is alleged to be responsible for the deaths of fifteen hundred of his fellow Salvadorians? And who belongs to a party that killed American Marines and AID contractors in what is called the Zona Rosa murders? What kind of neutrality is that? I don't know the answer to the question.

**DR. ANGEL RABASA:** I want to go back to this question of irregular warfare. I think it might be more accurate if the question had been posed in terms of asymmetric warfare, because what Chavez is doing is just that. At the high end, the Chavez government has purchased very advanced aircraft and other weapons systems from the Russians, but it also employs asymmetric warfare against Colombia and other targets of destabilization. Chavez and his supporters have developed a very sophisticated strategy of political warfare and we have seen that strategy at work in Bolivia. It is a combination of political violence with democratic methods or electoral methods to gain power. This method was inaugurated by the *piquiteros* (picketers) in Argentina. They would block roads, create chaos, and use violence to intimidate the opposition. Bolivian President Evo Morales mobilized thousands of supporters to besiege La Paz. And so there is a combination of that type of pressure with elections where the authoritarian leader manages to get himself elected and then proceeds to dismantle the institutions of democratic government. It is a very sophisticated method that allows Chavez supporters to come to power through ostensibly legal means and then they proceed to the consolidation of power.

**AMB. CURT WINSOR:** Again, I would say in response to both of my colleagues that they're right. But what is the underlying cause? The underlying cause is that the United States is not a player. We are not engaged in the region. So what you said is perfectly right. By the way, Bolivia is not immune nor has it had a history of nonviolence. They hung one of their presidents from a lamppost. This is nothing new

*A woman questions the legitimacy of the treatment of former Honduran President José Manuel Zelaya during the 2009 coup against him.*

**OTTO REICH:** Yes. As you very well know, there is no such article because that's a rhetorical question. The act that you describe has been declared a crime by the legal advisor of the armed forces. It wasn't the kidnapping of the president; it was the deportation of the president. Zelaya had already been removed by the Supreme Court. He had an order of arrest issued against him by a fifteen to zero vote of the Supreme Court, and there are plenty of articles in the Honduran constitution to support that ruling. I believe the article is 239. I said that in my testimony, when I testified back in July 2009. That's the exact article which enables all of the actions that took place against Zelaya to take place constitutionally. They don't have an impeachment process, by the way.

**FRANK GAFFNEY:** The deportation was unfortunate; he should have been thrown in jail. Yes, sir.

*A man asks about general long-term U.S. strategy in Latin America.*

**FRANK GAFFNEY:** Well, I'm not sure that I'm the best to answer that, but if I'm put on the spot, let me take a cut at it and others can chime in. I happen to think that the work that Nancy's Menges Project is doing, that brings us together annually now in these sessions, is trying to push the sorts of information that we're talking about here into the public domain to help translate it into political consequences. Not simply for informative purposes, but to actually have an impact from a policy point of view is the necessary first step. But it was obviously not sufficient. We have got to be taking the sorts of steps, if not necessarily normalization of drug trafficking, at least the kinds of things that I think we all would agree have to be addressed in terms of calling a spade a spade with respect to Hugo Chavez's regime as a state sponsor of terror. As Otto has described, the consequences that result from it could have the quite salutary effect of turning wishful thinking into reality, perhaps in the not-too-distant future. But here's the bottom line: as the president likes to say, "whether we like it or not," we have a border across which all of these problems flow. They flow in the forms of people coming here to flee despotism, or poverty, or both in many cases. They flow in the forms of illegal substances or materials, some of which could be very deadly not just to an individual consumer but to a population. It is an insecure border. It is a border that is, if anything, becoming more porous as the intensity of the effort to penetrate it, and the means by which it's being penetrated are ramping up.

So for all these reasons, we don't have the luxury of ignoring this. We will be hurt badly by it. And so I think the question is not so much what are we going to do about this as when are we going to do it? Are we really going to wait until that happens? We typically do. Can we afford to? I would suggest to you we cannot. Especially when, whether the Secretary of Defense acknowledges it or not, we have enemy armies now operating from safe havens in our hemisphere that we know have the capacity to bring weapons of mass destruction to bear. So the cost of waiting could be exceedingly high, and I pray that this kind of conversation and the work that the Menges Project and all these individuals are doing will translate into corrective action before that kind of horrible day arrives. Anybody else want to speak a little bit on that? If not, question? Yes, sir.

*A man asks a question about Columbia's operational success against the FARC.*

**DR. ANGEL RABASA:** The Colombians have developed a very sophisticated methodology to coordinate the actions of ministries and state agencies
to reestablish a state presence in areas recovered from the FARC and other
anti-social elements. One interesting thing about this framework is that it
was developed by the Colombians themselves. The origin of this initiative
was a class project at the Superior School of War. The members of the class
presented their project to the General Staff and then to the President who
approved it. So it is a Colombian product one hundred per cent.

The territorial consolidation process is divided into three stages. The
first stage is achieving territorial control. The goal is to take back control of a
particular area from the FARC. At this stage, the focus is on military operations, and the military has the main mission. The Colombians understand
that civil society, government institutions, education, and health services
cannot be brought in until there is security.

Once security is established—that is to say, once the main elements of
FARC are driven out of a particular area—then the transition moves to the
second stage: stabilization. This is the stage where the government controls
the area, but where there are residual elements of the FARC, for instance, the
militias that the FARC has in place to enforce its control. At this stage, the
focus is on providing security at the local level by using the police. So the primary mission shifts from the military to the police. A police presence is established to provide a sense of law and order and security to the population.
Also at this stage, there is the beginning of the provision of state services,
especially judicial functions.

The third stage is the consolidation stage. This is where the military
takes a very low profile and the primary role is taken by civilian agencies.
There is creation of infrastructure. The state attempts to develop the area ec-
onomically, to link it with the rest of the country, and to bring it educational
and health services.

These stages apply as well to the eradication of drugs. One of the reasons
for the lawlessness in these areas is that they are part of the drug economy.
In the first stage, the focus is on drug eradication, but the government
understands that it cannot just leave the coca farmers to their own devices.
The government provides emergency food for a period of ninety days. In the

second stage, the government provides seeds and fertilizers so that the former coca farmers can begin to develop subsistence agriculture. In the third stage, the government provides the assistance necessary to move the farmers from subsistence to commercial agriculture. So it's a very sophisticated process that involves the eventual fading out of the military as the primary player and the empowerment of the civil institutions of society.

**AMB. CURT WINSOR:** One of the factors that one looks at in Colombia is geography. There are few countries on earth with a more broken up territory than Colombia. Three ranges of the Andes Mountains intersect it.

Colombia is no stranger to violence. It had a cycle of violence, not much less than what we've been through recently, from 1948 through 1954, which ended with the dictatorship of Rojas Pinilla. A challenge for any government of Colombia is getting government to isolated areas of the country where you cannot use rail and there are few and difficult roads. Perhaps helicopters and other modes of transportation may make a difference there. But to talk about replacing cocaine with commercial crops for areas that are isolated from markets is part of the problem. Some fundamental solutions are needed that deal with the very unique problems of Colombia, which have to do with its geography, which is a contributing part to the difficulty of governing it.

**DR. ANGEL RABASA:** Can I just mention a quick comment in response to that? The Colombians know that. And they are putting the emphasis on secondary and tertiary roads so as to link these isolated locations to towns where they can sell their products. And then, of course, there is the linkage to the main road infrastructure system.

**FRANK GAFFNEY:** Could I say "thank you" to both this wonderful second panel and to our audience and of course, most especially, to Nancy Menges who has made all of this possible. This is a subject that we are serious about at the Center for Security Policy not only in terms of the here and now but going forward. So we appreciate your interest. We hope you'll help us translate this interest into policy impact for all the reasons that have been so well described here today. So thank you again for coming, and please check out the Center for Security Policy's website, securefreedom.org, for transcripts and video and other information that might be of use to you if you wish to help with this very important effort. Thank you.